Christian Wil~

Fundam

GABLER RESEARCH

Christian Willi Scheiner

Fundamental Determinants of Entrepreneurial Behaviour

GABLER

RESEARCH

Bibliographic information published by the Deutsche Nationalbibliothek
The Deutsche Nationalbibliothek lists this publication in the Deutsche Nationalbibliografie;
detailed bibliographic data are available in the Internet at http://dnb.d-nb.de.

Dissertation Universität Erlangen-Nürnberg, 2008

1st Edition 2009

Editorial Office: Claudia Jeske | Jutta Hinrichsen

Gabler is part of the specialist publishing group Springer Science+Business Media.
www.gabler.de

Umschlaggestaltung: KünkelLopka Medienentwicklung, Heidelberg
Printed on acid-free paper
Printed in Germany

ISBN 978-3-8349-1526-9

Foreword

In the academic field of entrepreneurship a multitude of research about the motives regarding the new venture creation has been conducted. But we still don't understand how people – especially students – develop their founding intentions. The knowledge about influencing factors that foster or impede this process and about differences between male and female entrepreneurs is also not sufficient.

In this remarkable book the author, Christian Scheiner, presents the results of several empirical studies which he recently conducted. Based on an innovative model which integrates proven theoretical concepts like "planned behaviour", "organisational socialisation", "gender theory" and "social learning", the author is able to identify main influencing factors upon the founding intentions of (potential) academic entrepreneurs. He also delivers empirical evidence that the founding motives as well as the intentions itself differ between German and British students.

These and many other empirical results that are presented and discussed in this book are finally transformed into recommendations of how to enhance entrepreneurial education, especially in universities. The author finally presents a survey of entrepreneurial initiatives that are already fostering the entrepreneurial activities of academic and non-academic founders in Germany.

Based on excellent research, this book offers new and innovative insights in the "early phases" of the new venture creation process. It can be highly recommended for researchers as well as practitioners who are engaged in the field of entrepreneurial education.

Prof. Dr. Kai-Ingo Voigt

Preface[1]

It is widely believed that the beginning is always the hardest part of any under-taking. Hence, some people revert to a little trick and write the introduction to their scientific dissertation at the end, because, in the beginning, thoughts and ideas are a bit of jumble and it is difficult to get a grasp on them and to establish some kind of order. Over time, the initial chaos becomes more structured, the focus is sharpened, what seemed too complex is suddenly comprehensible. Only at the end does one realise what is really important and where the focus lies. Writing a dissertation is similar in two aspects:

At the beginning of the dissertation, finding and approaching a suitable subject often seems to be an insurmountable barrier. At the end of this work, however, everything seems obvious and easy. Having said that, I would like to thank Prof. Dr. Kai-Ingo Voigt for supporting and encouraging me while also giving me the freedom I needed for my dissertation. I am grateful to my co-authors for the in-teresting co-operation. Thanks to our secretaries and student assistants for their support, Dietmar Katzer and Milena Goranova for their correction and editing efforts and to Prof. Dr. Nicole Koschate, who was the second supervisor.

In addition to topical aspects, the completion of a dissertation also marks the end of a defining period of life. At the onset of this new period, one is not sure what will happen. But as I said before, as time moves on, these things become clearer and easier. Without my family, friends and acquaintances, I would not have been able to write this dissertation. I would like to thank my colleagues, who were with me from the very beginning, these members of the "golden generation" Alex, Daniel, Lothar, Michael, Sascha and Stefanie. Your support and sense of humour made some things a lot easier for me. At the same time, I would like to thank Andi, Daliborka, Matthias, Sebastian and Tina.

---

[1] This book is written in British English. Appropriate rules regarding spelling, wording and grammar are applied. The author absolutely disagrees with all kinds of stereotyping by gender, race, nationality, ethnicity etc. However, to improve and simplify readability, party female and male indications for the appellation of persons are used, with no gender-related role typology being either stated or wanted. Even if only one kind of indication is used, always both genders are addressed.

Thanks to my supporters from outside the institute, particularly Milena, Frank, Max, Michi, Christian and Caro, who never tired of pointing out that there are more important things in life than work and my dissertation.

First and foremost I would like to thank my beloved father, my beloved mother and my dear sister Pia. Without you I would never have made it. I dedicate this dissertation to you as a symbol of my deep gratitude.

Christian Willi Scheiner

Glaubt man den Volksmund so stellt der Beginn von etwas immer das Schwierigste dar. Vielleicht wendet man deshalb einen kleinen Trick an und hebt sich. die Einleitung einer wissenschaftlichen Arbeit bis zum Schluss auf. Am Anfang kann man die Gedanken und Ideen nur schwer ordnen und greifen. Über die Zeit verschwindet die Unordnung und Komplexität und wird durch eine zunehmende Klarheit und Leichtigkeit abgelöst. Zudem weiß man erst am Ende, was das Bedeutende und Wichtige ist und worauf man gezielt hinweisen möchte. Das Verfassen einer Dissertation entspricht dem vor allem in zwei Aspekten:

Zu Beginn der Promotion scheint das Finden des Themas sowie die Auseinandersetzung damit eine unüberwindbare Hürde zu sein. Am Ende der Promotion hingegen kommt einem alles offensichtlich und einfach vor. In diesem Zusammenhang möchte ich Professor Dr. Kai-Ingo Voigt danken, der mir während der Promotion die notwendige Unterstützung und Betreuung sowie den erforderlichen Freiraum zuteil werden ließ. Bei meinen Koautoren möchte ich mich für die interessante Zusammenarbeit bedanken, bei unseren Sekretärinnen und studentischen Hilfskräften für ihre Unterstützung, bei Dietmar Katzer und Milena Goranova für die sprachliche Korrektur der Arbeit sowie bei Professorin Dr. Nicole Koschate für die Übernahme des Zweitgutachtens.

Neben dem themenbezogenem Aspekt stellt das Ende der Dissertation auch das Ende eines prägenden Lebensabschnitts dar, bei dem man am Anfang keine Ahnung von dem besitzt, was passieren und was sein wird. Aber wie bereits erwähnt, erlangt man auch in diesem Punkt eine Klarheit und Leichtigkeit. Ohne meine Familie, Freunde und Bekannten wäre diese Dissertation niemals so zustande gekommen. Beginnen möchte ich bei meinen Kollegen der ersten Stunde, der „goldenen Generation" Alex, Daniel, Lothar, Michael, Sascha und Stefanie, die mir mit ihrer Unterstützung und ihrem Humor vieles erleichtert haben. Gleichzeitig möchte ich aber auch Andi, Daliborka, Matthias, Sebastian und Tina nicht vergessen. Außerhalb des Lehrstuhls waren es vor allem Milena, Frank, Max, Michi, Christian und Caro, die mir immer wieder klar gemacht haben, dass es Wichtigeres als die Arbeit und meine Dissertation gibt.

Am meisten möchte ich mich bei meinem geliebten Papa, meiner geliebten Mama und meinem Schwesterherz Pia bedanken. Ohne Euch hätte ich das nie geschafft. Deshalb widme ich Euch die Dissertation aus Dankbarkeit für alles.

Christian Willi Scheiner

Contents

List of Figures

List of Tables

List of Abbreviations

AM   Average mean

FAU   Friedrich-Alexander-University

LL   Lower limit

SD   Standard deviation

Sig.   Significance

UL   Upper limit

1   Introduction

The main goal of this book is to create and advance the understanding of Entrepreneurship with regard to the determinants of and the exertion of influence on the development of entrepreneurial behaviour.

This doctoral thesis illustrates the result of extensive research during the last three years. The goal is to present an outstanding scientific work which shoes the qualification and ability of the author for a scientific work with an appropriate presentation. The doctoral thesis consists of selected key works, result of recent research, including a comprehensive framework and overview at the beginning.

The doctoral thesis is divided into six chapters. With exception of Chapter One, which is theoretical-conceptual, all further chapters are based on qualitative empirical research. Selected sections are written in cooperation with internal and external researchers.

To ensure high-quality research, the papers were submitted and presented at well-known international scientific conferences as well as being included into conference proceedings and a international renowned journals. For this reason, five out of six papers have run through various triple- and double-blind peer-review processes.

Partly based on the feedback of reviewers and at various conferences, each presented chapter besides Chapter Five is, in its form and contents, completely revised by the author.

In the following, each chapter will be partly introduced.

Chapter 2: Fundamental Determinants of Entrepreneurial Behaviour

In this chapter an own theoretical framework for further considerations will be developed. Therefore, the theory of planned behaviour will be combined with social learning theory, organisational socialisation and gender theory.

This framework will server as an overall theoretical framework and thematically linkage between the following chapters.

Chapter 3: Gender-related Differences in Founding Intentions

Since 2006, there has been a research cooperation between the University of Erlangen-Nuremberg (Chair of Industrial Management, Prof. Dr. Kai-Ingo Voigt) and the European Business School Reichartshausen (Chair of Entrepreneurship, Prof. Dr. Heinz Klandt). One outcome is this research paper, submitted and presented at the 29th Babson College Entrepreneurship Research Conference in Chapel Hill (USA)[2] Furthermore a version of this paper was published in 'Journal of Asia Entrepreneurship and Sustainability' (Vol. IV. Issue 4) in 2009.

Chapter 4: Gender-related Differences in Motivation, Goals and Performance?

This chapter is based on a paper that was submitted and presented at the 29th Babson College Entrepreneurship Research Conference in Chapel Hill (USA).[1]

---

[2] These papers are based on a collaboration between the University of Erlangen-Nuremberg and the European Business School. In this collaboration worked Stavroula Laspiate (European Business School Reichartshausen), Alexander Brem (University of Erlangen-Nuremberg), Simone Chlosta (European Business School Reichartshausen), Prof. Dr. Kai-Ingo Voigt (University of Erlangen-Nuremberg), Prof. Dr. Heinz Klandt (European Business School Reichartshausen) together. The papers were written in different compositions.

Chapter 5: Students' Attitude towards Entrepreneurship: Does Gender Matter?

This chapter is based on two different articles submitted and presented at the Internationalizing Entrepreneurship Education and Training (IntEnt) 17th Global Conference with the conference theme 'Innovative Formats for Entrepreneurship Education Teaching'[1] in July 2007 (Poland) and European Council for Small Business and Entrepreneurship (ECSB) 52nd World Conference with the conference theme 'At the Crossroads of East and West: New Opportunities fir Entrepreneurship and Small Business' in June 2007 in Turku (Finland). Furthermore, the present version of the paper was published in the Journal 'Review of International Comparative Management' (Vol. 8, Issue 4) in 2007.[1]

Chapter 6: Entrepreneurship Education in the United Kingdom and Germany

Since 2006, there has been a research cooperation between the University of Erlangen-Nuremberg (Chair of Industrial Management, Prof. Dr. Kai-Ingo Voigt) and the Leeds Metropolitan University. One outcome of this cooperation is this research paper, submitted and presented at the and at the 30th Institute for Small Business & Entrepreneurship Conference(ISBE) in November 2007 (Scotland)[3].

Chapter 7: Foundation and Development Support for Business Start-ups and Small Enterprises in Germany

This chapter is based on article submitted and presented at the 53rd World Conference of the International Council for Small Business (ICSB) with the conference theme 'Advancing Small Business and Entrepreneurship: From Research to Results' in June 2008 (Canada).

---

[3] Together with Ted Sarmiento (Leeds Metropolitan University), Alexander Brem (University of Erlangen-Nuremberg) and Prof. Dr. Kai-Ingo Voigt (University of Erlangen-Nuremberg).

Chapter 8: Concluding Remarks

In this chapter an overall conclusion is drawn as well as implications for practice and empirical and further research shown.

2 Fundamental Determinants of Entrepreneurial Behaviour

2.1 Introduction

According to Scase and Goffee (1980) the conventional thinking about how entrepreneurial ideas, intention and behaviour emanate in a society is so complex and individual that it lies beyond analysis. Being and becoming an entrepreneur was attributed to something almost inborn and inherited (Gibb & Ritchie, 1982). It was argued that some psychological characteristics exist that are shared by entrepreneurs (Brockhaus, 1982) which illustrate a main research objective. A major stream in academic entrepreneurship research has been focussed on determining psychological characteristics that are associated with entrepreneurs and factors that encourage them to start a business (Rauch & Frese, 2007; Scherer et al., 1989).

It was further argued that this personality profile of entrepreneurs would differ from the one of the general population on factors as risk-taking propensity (e.g. Petrakis, 2005; Sexton & Bowman, 1983; McClelland, 1961; Welsh & White, 1981; Palmer, 1971; Timmons, 1978), locus of control orientation (e.g. Borland, 1975; Brockhaus & Nord, 1979) and achievement motivation (e.g. Sexton & Bowmann, 1983; Bowen & Hisrich, 1986; DeCarlo & Lyons, 1979). In addition, a multitude of normative and descriptive studies attributed characteristics such as need for achievement (e.g. Liles 1974, Hornaday & Aboud 1971), need for power (e.g. Winter, 1973; Hartmann, 1959), desire for responsibility (Welsh & White, 1981; Sutton, 1995; Davids, 1963) to the entrepreneur. Carland et al. (1984) and Gartner (1988) have presented an excellent overview of identified characteristics (see table 1).

Bearing in mind those numerous identified characteristics, it can be argued that this plethora on findings, that are even not stable when they are compared, impede or illustrate a major obstacle to find a common understanding of an entrepreneur and hence, for a common definition of the term entrepreneur itself. A focus only on traits to describe an entrepreneur is likely to be almost useless in building a common knowledge (e.g. Sexton & Smilor 1985; Casrud et al., 1985; Gartner, 1988).

Table 1: Characteristics of entrepreneurs

Author(s)	Characteristics	Norma-tive	Empiri-cal
Davids	Ambition; desire for independence; re-sponsibility; self confidence		x
Dunkelberg and Cooper	Growth oriented; independence oriented		x
Durand	Achievement motivation; locus of control; training		x
Gasse	Personal value orientation		x
Hartmann	Source of formal authority	x	
Hisrich and O'Brien	Self discipline and perseverance; desire to succeed, action orientation; goal orienta-tion; energy level		x
Hornaday and Aboud	Need for achievement; autonomy: aggres-sion; power; recognition; innova-tive/independent		x
Hornady and Bunker	Need for achievement; intelligence; crea-tivity; energy level; taking initiative; self-reliance; leadership; desire for money; recognition desire; accomplishment drive; power affiliation; tolerance of uncertainty		x
Liles	Need for achievement		x
McClelland	Risk taking, need for achievement		x
Mill	Risk bearing	x	
Palmer	Risk management		x
Schumpeter	Innovation, initiative	x	/
Sexton	Energetic/ambitious; positive reaction set-backs		x
Sutton	Desire for responsibility	x	
Timmons	Drive/self-confidence, goal orientated moderated risk taker; internal locus of control; creativity/innovation	x	x
Wainer and Rubin	Achievement; power affiliation		x
Welsh and White	Need to control; responsibility seeker; self-confidence/drive; challenge taker; moderate risk taker		x
Winter	Need for power	x	

Source: Following Carland et al. (1984) and Gartner (1988)

Well supported theoretical frameworks from different research areas and disci-plines can be adapted to give support to the conceptual development of entrepre-neurial studies. In this context, Scherer et al. (1989) point out that the "use of

behavioural and social psychology theories presents an opportunity to move entrepreneurship research from its rich descriptive history to more scientific goals
of explanations and prediction" (p. 17). Consequently, the perspective on entrepreneurship research is drawn from the question "what is an entrepreneur" to the
question "what influences people to develop entrepreneurial behaviour" (e.g.
Carsrud & Johnson, 1989; Scherer et al, 1990) respectively "what are the antecedents of entrepreneurial behaviour". Thus, factors have to be examined that lead
to entrepreneurial activity.

The majority of research in entrepreneurship however has concentrated on entrepreneurs during their professional activities. Hence, research mainly starts with
the decision to start a business or the foundation itself (e.g. Hisrich & O'Brien,
1981; Voigt & Brem, 2006; Renzulli et al., 2000; Hisrich & O'Brien, 1982; Rosa
& Hamilton, 1994; Voigt et al., 2007; Man et al., 2008). The phase before the
entrepreneurial behaviour has not attracted the same attention. To predict and to
influence people in their decision to become an entrepreneur, exactly the phase
before the entrepreneurial behaviour takes place, offers essential insights for researcher and educators. Therefore, it is important to understand the fundamental
determinants of entrepreneurial behaviour. In this chapter a theoretical framework will be created that links social learning theory, organisational socialisation
and gender theory with the theory of planned behaviour

2.2 Entrepreneurship and Entrepreneur

Entrepreneurship comprises a multitude of different aspects (Fallgatter, 2002)
that makes it complicated to define "entrepreneurship" and "entrepreneur" unitar-
ily. In fact, definitions of "entrepreneurship" and "entrepreneur" are characterised by a vast heterogeneity.

To define entrepreneurship mainly a process-oriented perspective has been chosen by researchers (e.g. Bygrave, 1989; Kuratko & Hodgetts, 1998; Stevenson &
Jarillo, 1990; Timmons, 1999). Hisrich and Peters (1998) see entrepreneurship as
a process of creating something new. Necessary time and effort have to be in-
vested and financial, psychic and social risks to be taken. As a result, personal
satisfaction and independence as well as monetary reward are received. Stevenson and Jarillo (1990) point at the circumstance that entrepreneurship is not only
limited to ownership but it can also take place both inside and outside of organisations. Other authors like Low and Abrahmson (1997) have a more simple defi-

nition. They argue that entrepreneurship illustrates the creation of an organisation. Another approach is suggested by Gibb (1987). He refers to entrepreneurship "as the marked use of combination of these attributes in pursuit of a particular task, usually in an industrial or commercial context" (p. 11). Curran and
Stanworth (1989) emphasise that entrepreneurship is describing the creation of a
new economic entity that is centred on a new service or product: the service or
product does not have to be completely new but it has to differ from existing offers in content, marketing and/or organisational configuration. The definition of
Kuratko and Hodgetts (1998) is seen as the most appropriate one in the context
of this doctoral thesis. They define entrepreneurship "as a process of innovation
and new venture creation through four major dimensions – individual, organisational, environmental, process – that is aided by collaborative networks in government, education, and institutions. All of the macro and micro positions of entrepreneurial thought must be considered while recognising and seizing opportunities that can be converted in to marketable ideas capable of competing for implementation for today's economy" (p. 47).

The term entrepreneur was already used in the sixteenth century but in the twen-
tieth century the meaning changed towards the entrepreneur as an inventor and
innovator (Fallgater, 2002). From a historical point of development, Mill and
Schumpeter should be mentioned. Mill is considered to be the first author in scientific literature who used and promoted the term entrepreneur among econo-
mists. Schumpeter also belongs to the pioneers in this scientific field who emphasised that the role of innovation would define an entrepreneur (1934). Similar
to the concept of entrepreneurship, a multitude of different definitions for the
term entrepreneur have been developed in scientific literature since the first establishment in research. Depending on the taken perspective or scientific disci-
pline entrepreneur describes different circumstances. The description of Vesper
(1990) illustrates an excellent summary in this context: "To an economist, an entrepreneur is one who brings resources, labour, materials, and other assets into
combinations that make their value greater than before, and also one who intro-
duces changes, innovations and a new order. ... The unfavourably inclined politician may see an entrepreneur as one who is devious and hard to control,
whereas a favourably inclined politician sees the same person as one who finds
effective ways to get things done. To a businessperson, the same entrepreneur
may be an ally, source of supply, a customer, or someone good to invest in. To a

communist philosopher, the entrepreneur may be a predator, one who usurps resources and exploits the labour of others. The same person is seen by a capitalist philosopher as one who creates wealth for others as well, who finds better ways to utilize resources, and reduce waste, and who produces jobs others are glad to get" (p. 2). In general and in the context of this dissertation, an entrepreneur is seen as someone who develops and applies entrepreneurial behaviour.

2.3 Intention Models as Base of the Theoretical Framework

2.3.1 Intention Models

With the shift in scientific literature from the question "what is an entrepreneur" to "what influences people to develop entrepreneurial behaviour" (e.g. Carsrud & Johnson 1989, Scherer et al, 1990), respectively "what are the antecedents of entrepreneurial behaviour", theories from psychological literature gained on importance because they emphasised that intentions are predictors of activity and have to be examined. The work of Fishbein and Ajzen (1975) played therein an essential role. They described the correlation as an evolutionary transition from beliefs to attitudes, from attention to intention and finally from intention to behaviour. The development of behaviour can consequently be understood as somehow determined or planned.

Even if the finding of an idea can be an act of creativity and inspiration, the foundation of a business is nothing unconscious and unintended (Bird, 1988). Therefore, Bird (1988) and Katz and Gartner (1988) argue that entrepreneurship is a type of planned behaviour. In psychology, intentions have proven to be the best predictor for planned behaviour, when that behaviour is hard to observe, rare, or involves time lags that can not be predicted (Krueger et al., 2000). Entrepreneurial behaviour fulfils exactly these characteristics. Intention models can subsequently contribute significantly to gain insights into entrepreneurship and to increase the understanding of the fundamental determinants of entrepreneurship. Based on such insights a more sophisticated entrepreneurship education approaches can be created.

Several researchers have developed intention models (Peterman & Kennedy, 2003). The dominant models were developed by Bird (1988), Boyd and Vozikis (1994) and Ajzen (1991). Those models are largely homogeneous.

2.3.1.1 Intention Model of Bird

Bird (1988) defines intention as "a state of mind directing a person's attention (and therefore experience and action) toward a specific object (goal) or a path in order to achieve something (means)" (p.422). Bird (1988) further assumes that entrepreneurial intention directs e.g. the goal setting, commitment, communication, development and growth from the beginning. In her model personal and contextual factors antecede entrepreneurial intention. Personal factors comprise personal history, personality and ability. Contextual factors consist of social, political and economic variables. Intention is, in addition, influenced by rational, analytical and cause-effect thinking and intuitive, holistic and contextual thinking (see figure 1).

Figure 1: Bird's intention model

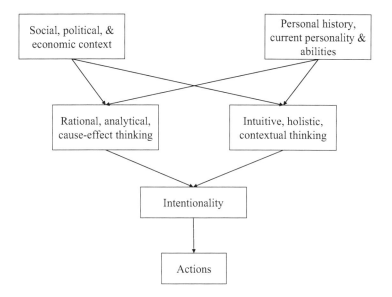

Source: Bird (1988), p. 444.

2.3.1.2 Intention Model of Boyd and Vozikis

Boyd and Vozikis (1994) took Bird's intention model and developed it further. Intention is for them "based on the way in which people perceive their social and physical environment, as well as the way in which they anticipate the future outcomes of their behaviour" (p. 69). Perceived expectations, attitudes, situations, beliefs, and preferences have an influence on the development of intentions. These perceptions are further factors affected by unique, individual perceived occurrences in the past. Individuals develop a repertory of stored pieces of information that are result of their history (Boyd & Vozikis, 1994; Ryan, 1970) which means that they are result of the personal and contextual variables. Their model further includes that rational and intuitive thinking influences the behavioural intention and the entrepreneurial activity. The main development of Bird's intention model is the integration of self-efficacy. Self-efficacy illustrates the confidence of an individual in his or her ability to perform behaviour (Bandura, 1977). It is an outcome of these cognitive thought processes and the development is influenced by "mastery experiences, observational learning, social persuasion, and perceptions of physiological well-being that have been derived from the personal and contextual variables" (Boyd & Vozikis 1994, p. 69). Attitudes and self-efficacy concerning the probability of a failure or success subsequently have an effect on the development of entrepreneurial intention. Self-efficacy also functions as a moderator between intention and activity. Hence, a high degree of self-efficacy illustrates a basic prerequisite for the transition from intention to activity (see figure 2).

Figure 2: Boyd and Vozikis' intention model

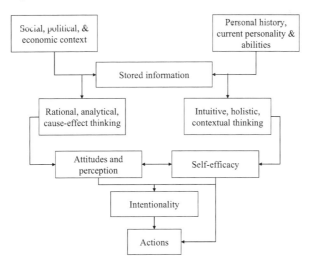

Source: Boyd & Vozikis (1994), p. 69.

Within this dissertation the intention model of Ajzen (1991) will be the base and starting point for the development of a theoretical framework. Therein, the theoretical base for the fundamental determinants of entrepreneurship will be laid.

2.3.1.3 Theory of Planned Behaviour of Ajzen

The theory of planned behaviour is rooted in the theory of reasoned action (Fishbein & Ajzen, 1975; Ajzen & Fishbein, 1980). The theory of reasoned action postulates that "behavioural intentions are a function of salient information and beliefs about the likelihood that performing a particular behaviour will lead to a specific outcome" (Madden et al., 1992, p. 3). These beliefs consist of normative and behavioural beliefs as a conceptually distinct set. Normative beliefs influence the subjective norm of an individual about performing this behaviour. Behavioural beliefs are the underlying influence on the attitude of an individual towards performing a specific behaviour (Madden et al., 1992). Hence, salient information and beliefs impact intentions and finally behaviour through subjective norms and/or attitude. External variables which are not included into the model influence intention indirectly by affecting the subjective norms and attitudes (see figure 3).

Figure 3: Theory of reasoned action

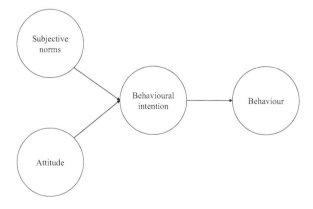

Source: Madden et al. (1992), p. 4.

In the theory of planned behaviour (see figure 4) illustrates the individual intention as well an essential and fundamental factor to perform a given behaviour. Motivational factors, that influence behaviour, are assumed to be captured by intention (Ajzen, 1991). They are "indicators of how hard people are willing to try, of how much of an effort they are planning to exert, in order to perform a behaviour. ... [The] stronger the intention to engage in a behaviour, the more likely should be its performance" (p. 181). The stronger the intention to become self-employed, the more likely is the foundation of a business. A prerequisite however is that the behaviour is under the volitional control of an individual. It should be stated that the performance of most behaviours depend at least to a certain extent on non-motivational factors. Such factors refer to the availability of resources and opportunities (Ajzen, 1991). The actual control over a specific behaviour is a combination of both factors. More important than the actual control is, however, the perceived behavioural control by the individual. Perceived behavioural control resembles the concept of self-efficacy of Bandura (1977). The integration of perceived behavioural control is in fact the main difference between the theory of reasoned behaviour and the theory of planned behaviour. In summary, the theory of planned behaviour argues that the probability for actual behaviour is related to the extent to which an individual intends to perform this behaviour and perceives his/her behavioural control. Both factors can be used to predict directly behaviour (Ajzen, 1991).

Figure 4: Theory of planned behaviour

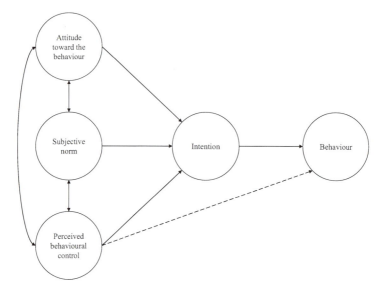

Source: Ajzen (1991), p. 182.

2.4   Social Learning Theory

2.4.1   Social Learning Theory

Perceived behavioural control, respectively self-efficacy, has been identified as a main component of Ajzen's theory of planned behaviour. The concept of self-efficacy belongs to the social learning theory. The social learning theory goes back to the work of Bandura in 1968 and was further developed by e.g. Bandura (1977), Mahoney (1974), Mischel (1973) and Davis and Luthans (1979, 1980). The social learning theory offers deeper insights into the effect-cause relations of the theory of planned behaviour and answers the questions "what influences people to develop entrepreneurial behaviour" and "what are the antecedents of entrepreneurial behaviour".

Social learning theory is derived from the emphasis on learning from other people (Davis & Luthans, 1980) and belongs to the behavioural theory. The core idea of the social learning theory is that behaviour is a result from the interaction of situations and persons. It combines principles of operant classical conditioning with cognitive-based dispositional determinants of a person's behaviour (Ginter & White, 1982).

Rudimentary, learning which is directly based on experience, results from positive and negative effects that are linked to actions. Some actions are rewarded; some have no effect or lead to a punishing outcome. This process of different reinforcements can lead to the selection of successful forms of behaviour and abandonment of unsuccessful or ineffective forms. Learning by reinforcement can be understood as a mechanistic process "in which responses are shaped automatically and unconsciously by their immediate consequences" (Bandura, 1977, p. 17). The cognitive capacity of humans enables them to gain to a higher degree from experiences. Three different functions are associated with response consequences (Bandura, 1977):

- They communicate pieces of information.

- They can motivate through their incentive value.

- They strengthen responses automatically.

If learning, however, would rely solely on the effects of actions, it would be excessively exertive and risky. Fortunately, human behaviour is mostly learned by observation through modelling. Thus, a human being observes the actions of others, develops an idea how this new behaviour is carried out, and uses this information as a guide for own action. The advantage of this procedure is that errors can be avoided by the adaptation of observed behaviour (Bandura, 1977).

The process of observational learning is regulated by the interrelated four sub processes of "attentional processes", "retention processes", "motor reproduction processes" and "motivational processes" (Bandura, 1977) (see figure 5). Attentional process focuses on the fact that a human being is not able to learn much by observation if he or she is not vigilant and perceives the significant aspects of the modelled behaviour not in an accurate way. Retention process addresses that people can just be influenced by the observation of modelled behaviour if they can remember it. Motor reproduction processes, as a third component, highlights that new behaviour is learned by the combination of observation and a trial-and-error approach. New behaviour is thus achieved by modelling and by self-corrective adjustments. Motivational processes emphasise that people are more likely to adopt modelled behaviour if the probable outcome leads to a rewarded or unrewarded effect.

Figure 5: Component processes governing observational learning in the social learning analysis

Source: Bandura (1977), p. 23.

Social learning theory relies, hence, heavily on the mediating effects of covert cognitive processes, as almost every aspect of social learning is seen to be affected by cognitive processes (Davis & Luthans, 1980). Bandura (1977) points out in this context, that "most external influences affect behaviour through intermediary cognitive processes. Cognitive factors partly determine which external events will be observed, how they will be perceived, whether they leave any lasting effects, what valence and efficacy they have, and how the information they convey will be organised for future use" (p. 160). Notably, before researchers like Bandura (1969) and Staats (1968) have demonstrated the importance of covert cognitions for the regulation of human behaviour, the issue has been almost neglected in scientific research (Davis & Luthans, 1980).

With cognition as fundamental basis, social learning theory sees a person operating in a state of interactive reciprocal determinism with the environment and behaviour (Davis & Luthans, 1980) (see figure 6). As every aspect influences the other, Mahoney (1977) argues that the actual existing environment can differ in the perception from individual to individual due to the cognition.

Figure 6: Model of social learning

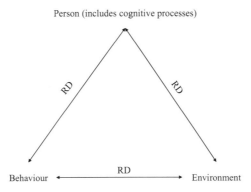

RD = reciprocal determinism

Source: Ginter & White (1982), p. 255.

2.4.2 Social Learning and Entrepreneurial Behaviour Development

Social learning theory can contribute to the explanation of why people develop entrepreneurial behaviour. The development of entrepreneurial behaviour can occur when an individual observes a valued model and notices that this model becomes involved into numerous and different behaviours which lead to positive reinforcements. The observer then evaluates the reinforcement. If the potential reinforcement is valued, he or she will try to imitate the model's behaviour to receive similar reinforcements (Bandura, 1977). Scherer et al. (1989) use this explanatory correlation and transfer it to the development of entrepreneurial be-haviour. They argue that children learn in their socialisation process – which takes mainly place in the framework of the family environment – specific social norms, customs, attitudes and educational practices by observing their models respectively parents. As a result a child develops reinforced behaviours on the formed habit hierarchy. This habit hierarchy is called personality or enduring characteristics of behaviour (Scherer et al., 1989).

2.4.3 Social Learning Theory and Entrepreneur Career Selection

In addition, Krumboltz et al. (1976) used the social learning theory to answer specifically the question "why do people happen to enter a particular educational programmes or occupations they do" (p. 71). Thus, the career selection process was analysed. They offer a theoretical framework within which the selection of a specific career can be examined. According to Krumboltz et al. (1976) four categories would influence this career decision:

- Generic endowment and special abilities

- Environmental conditions and events

- Learning experiences

- Task approach skills

Generic endowment and special abilities affect the inborn and inherited abilities and qualities. These abilities and qualities can set limits on the educational and occupational preferences, selections and skills (e.g. sex). Environmental conditions and events as second category comprises factors, that are usually outside of the individual sphere of influence, but have impact on the decision making process. Among others Krumboltz et al. (1976) use family training experiences and resources as an example for this category. Each family teaches the child different things and provides – according to the availability – different resources. Learning experiences illustrate the third category. Even if Krumboltz et al. (1976) state that especially this category is confronted with the fact that "patterns of stimuli and reinforcement, their nature and scheduling are so exceedingly complex that no theory can adequately account for the infinite variations that influence the development of career preferences" (p. 72), two simplified learning categories are described. Instrumental learning experiences describe the behaviour of an individual to generate certain consequences or rewards. Associative learning experiences comprise observational learning by individuals from a real or imaginary model and the motor reproduction process. If an individual is confronted with an inexperienced problem he or she uses its task approach skills (fourth category), which have an effect on the outcome. Thereafter, the task approach skills are modified.

Bearing in mind the general principles of social learning theory in the context of the career selection process it is suggested that career and occupational role models are an important environmental factor for the career choice (Scherer et al., 1989). An individual is more likely to choose entrepreneurship as career path, if

an observational learning from a valued model happens, that is engaged success-
fully in activities related to self-employment. In the cognitive process of social
learning the individuals evaluate whether success can be achieved in this career
path. At the same time, the individual examines whether necessary competencies
exist or can be acquired to be successful in this kind of career. Hence, the individual can be either encouraged or discouraged to enter this specific path of a
career. The influence of parents as model is assumed to be a powerful determinant (Scherer et al., 1989). Hence, a child could in general come to the conclusion that the self-employment career of the parents is an option worth striving
for. The child with a family background in which one or both parents are de-
pendent-employed, could convince the child to seek another career path as the
existing and perceived reinforcements are not valued by the child. This correlation could also exist vice versa. The antecedents of intention and intention itself
to become an entrepreneur are, thus, influenced by the social learning results.
Figure 7 summarises the entrepreneurial development from a social learning perspective.

Figure 7: Process of entrepreneurial career choice from a social learning perspective

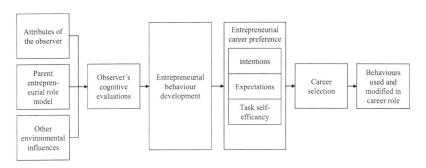

Source: Following Scherer et al. (1989), p. 22.

The influence of family background, especially the influence of the father or
mother, on the entrepreneurial career choice has been empirically found in scientific research. Several studies support that family background is linked to the
propensity to choose self-employment as a career (Scott & Twomey, 1988;
Römer-Paakkanen & Rauhala, 2007; Wang & Wong, 2004; Benett & Dann,
2000). Singh and DeNoble (2003) for example showed that a close self-
employed relative has, among other factors, a strong positive impact on the

attitude on self-employment. Moreover, Klandt (1984) found in his study that the father's profession has an effect on the occupational decision of the son and the daughter, while the mother's influence is mostly limited to the daughter. According to DeMartino and Barbato (2003) women are more influenced by the family background to found a business than men.

2.4.4 Social Learning in the Theoretical Framework

Social learning theory helps to identify and to understand the fundamental determinants of entrepreneurial behaviour and activity. It addresses the questions "what influences people to develop entrepreneurial behaviour" and "why do people choose entrepreneurship as career choice". Individuals perceive and evaluate behaviour in their social environment and use this to examine whether offered reinforcements result in an adjustment and development of specific habit hierarchy, respectively personality. This shapes the beliefs, attitude and intention of an individual. At the same time, social learning theory illustrates how the choice to become an entrepreneur is influenced by the observation and evaluation of model's career choice. Especially the family background and the socialisation, which mainly occurs in the family environment, have a major influence and importance on the social learning process. Figure 8 includes social learning theory into the theoretical framework with the theory of planned behaviour as a basis.

Figure 8: Social learning theory as part of the theoretical framework

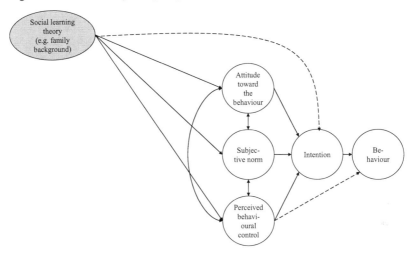

2.5   Organisational Socialisation

2.5.1 Organisational Socialisation

Social learning theory argues that entrepreneurial behaviours and career choices can be learned and influenced. Entrepreneurial activity is thus not solely inherited and inborn but something which can be influenced and taught (Kuratko, 2006). Bearing this in mind, organisations can try to exert influence on their members in order to develop entrepreneurial behaviour among them. In the context of this chapter the efforts and approaches of the university as kind of organisation will be examined with regard to the development of entrepreneurial attitude, intention and behaviour among students. Especially the role of the entrepreneurship education as a tool for this outcome will be examined. Bowen (1981) points out that education in general is the medium of society to transfer and implement its ideas. The education process represents, hence, a form of socialisation. As the considered socialisation in this dissertation occurs in and is determined by universities, entrepreneurship education illustrates a form of organisational socialisation.

"At the heart of organisational socialisation is a jejune phrase used by social scientists to refer to the process by which one is taught and learns "the ropes" of a particular organisational role. In its most general sense, organisational socialisation is then the process by which an individual acquires the social knowledge and skills necessary to assume an organisational role" (Van Maanen & Schein, 1977, p. 3). In addition, commonsensical beliefs, principles, norms and attitudes shall be transferred on the individual. The expected roles which shall be created and passed on by members of the organisation include simultaneously process characteristics, which refer to the question "how should people do something?", and content characteristics, which refer to the question "what should people do?". Thus, an organisational, cultural perspective is established, so that new members in the organisation see the organisational world in a similar way like their experienced members (Van Maanen & Schein, 1977). Expected behaviour is reinforced while unexpected and unwanted behaviour is not rewarded or even punished. Van Maanen and Schein (1977) use the phrase "organisational socialisation process" to illustrate the manner in which this teaching/learning is taking place. Within universities numerous socialisation processes occur. Each faculty tries to transfer a culture on its members. In the medical faculty, in the context of medicine as subculture of a university for example, sick people shall be healed by applying appropriate treatment based on a sophisticated diagnosis. In the context of entrepreneurship education it means that students, academics and professors develop entrepreneurial attitudes, intention and finally behaviour.

2.5.2 Entrepreneurship Education as Form of Organisational Socialisation

2.5.2.1 The Framework of Entrepreneurship Education

Entrepreneurship education is solely configured and determined by universities. Universities are embedded in a macro-environment which influences the entrepreneurship education activities. Pittaway and Cope (2007) developed on the basis of a systematic literature review a thematic framework of entrepreneurship education (see figure 9) that summarises drives and influencing variables of entrepreneurship education. The first macro-level consists of the general policy climate for entrepreneurship education, the promotion, measurement and funding of such education. The second macro-level comprises the university enterprise context. Therein, the general enterprise infrastructure, the university commercialisation policies and the supply of faculty are included. The interface between the university and other organisations indicates the next level. Academic enterprise, management training, outreach activities and student-entrepreneur-interactions can be found in this level. These contextual factors describe the indirect inputs into entrepreneurship education. The core of entrepreneurship education is the programme context as it is the direct input of entrepreneurship education. Pittaway and Cope (2007) subsume here exemplarily pedagogy in the curriculum, extra-curricula activity, departmental philosophies, student orientation and propensity as well as student capability. The entrepreneurial activity from students, graduates and the graduate recruitment shows the final category.

Figure 9: Framework of entrepreneurship education

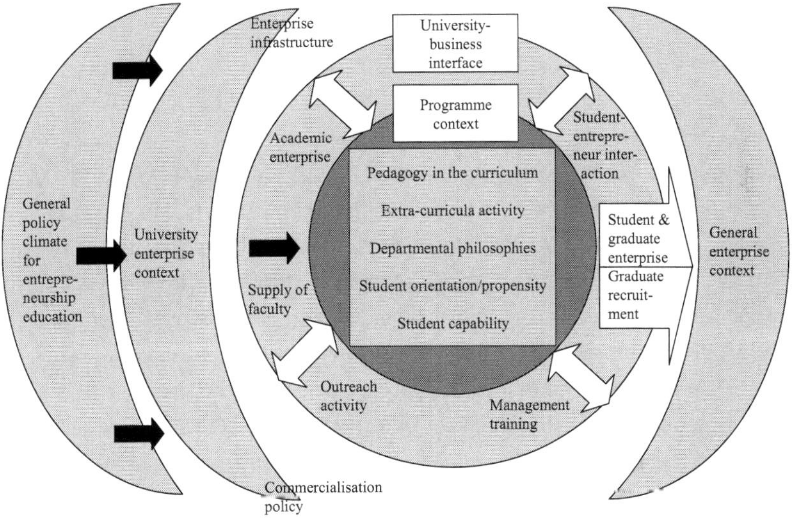

Source: Pittaway & Cope (2007), p. 484.

2.5.2.2 Entrepreneurship Education in the Academic Environment

The possibility of entrepreneurship education to effectuate entrepreneurial attitude, intention and behaviour is strongly dependent on entrepreneurship on its recognition and status as aim of science and university education.

The generic relevance of entrepreneurship education is not always recognised as general aim of science. In universities it is still often distinguished between the search for truth in science, respectively the generation of knowledge on one side, and search for invention on the other, as possible aims of science. Merton (1963) for example sees "universalism", "communism", "disinterestedness" and "organised scepticism" as the normative structure of science. From this point of view the search for truth and knowledge for its own sake is considered as the veritable function of a university (Merton, 1968). The search for inventions, in contrast, is sometimes associated as an inappropriate focus on ideas that have potential practical and above all commercial applicability (Louis et al., 1998). The perception of universities has, however, changed. Universities are an essential element for technological development and economic growth. Klofsten and Evans (2000) summarise this by stating that an "academic institution is no longer considered as being an isolated island of knowledge" (p. 299). Universities are rather seen as a drive of economic growth, a source of employment and income, and a centre for cultural life.

Addressing the purpose of university education, entrepreneurship education is further doubted to be legitimate. It could be even argued that entrepreneurship education has, almost per se, "the potential to clash with deep-rooted conceptions about the proper conduct of university, even business school education" (Laukkanen, 2000, p.27). In general two different opinions can be found. Proponents of the liberal perspective argue that education aims at teaching students about their responsibilities as members of society and about moral concepts (e.g. equality, liberty) (e.g. Corson, 2000; Hirst, 1974). The preparation of students with skills and competencies to fulfil business or changing economic demands is denied. Instead, education should cultivate a value system to turn students into informed citizens. Thereupon it would be possible for them to make meaningful contributions to their community and society (Myrah & Currie, 2006). The contrary position is taken by the vocational theorists. They postulate that students should be prepared for the world of work (esp. entrepreneurship) (Sage, 1993; Warwick, 1998). Entrepreneurship is valued as "subject worthy of study because it fosters skills such as enterprise, creativity and flexibility; skills that are deemed essential for succeeding in the current and future marketplace" (Myrah & Currie, 2006, p. 235). In practice, a compromise of both perspectives can been found, even if the liberal-vocational debate has not ended. The compromise sees a functional orientation in education with informed and responsibly acting students as an aim.

The reason for this compromise is correlated with a shift of governmental attitudes on local, regional, national and European level towards the role of universities as a central drive of economic development. Governments admonish universities to commercialise their scientific results, to create an entrepreneurial climate and culture as well as to be entrepreneurial. Furthermore, several programmes (e.g. EXIST) have been established to support universities in their effort to fulfil given, own and public expectations and requirements.

2.5.2.3 Objectives of Entrepreneurship Education

Even if the first course of entrepreneurship education was held for the first time in the United States of America more than 60 years ago (Katz, 2002), no common, unitary understanding of the term entrepreneurship education exists in the scientific literature.

Depending on the perspective taken on entrepreneurship education, different definitions can be found. Gottleib and Ross (1997) define entrepreneurship education in terms of innovation and creativity applied to governmental, business and social fields. Kourilsky (1995) sees opportunity recognition, building a business venture and marshalling of resources in risk-afflicted environments and situations as characteristics of entrepreneurship education. Brinks (2005) links entrepreneurship education to "the pedagogical process involved in the encouragement of entrepreneurial activities, behaviours and mindsets from the point of insight and creativity at the outset to innovation and progress when fully implemented. In short, it covers all aspects of the route from brain to market and more generally from brain to improvement and progress" (p. 2). Based on Garavan et al. (1995) Hynes (1996) states that entrepreneurship education is "the process or series of activities which aims to enable an individual to assimilate and develop knowledge, skills values and understand that are not simply related to a narrow field of activity, but which allow a broad range of problems to be defined, analysed and solved" (p. 10).

As numerous the definitions of entrepreneurship as many objectives of entrepreneurship education can be found. Hills (1988) identified three main objectives. Firstly, awareness has to be increased and understanding has to be created with regard to how to initiate and manage a business start-up. Secondly, students have to be made aware that small business ownership illustrates a career option. Thirdly, a fuller understanding of the interrelationships between the functional areas has to be developed. Hytti and O'Goreman (2004) propose three objectives. The first one is to develop a broad understanding of entrepreneurship which comprises the role of entrepreneurs and entrepreneurship in modern societies. As a second objective, they see the importance of becoming entrepreneurial. This aspect deals with the need of individuals to take the responsibility for their own career, life and learning. The third objective is for individuals to learn how to be an entrepreneur, respectively how to start a business. Solomon et al. (2002) have a different approach and argue that a core objective of entrepreneurship education is to be different from the typical business education as business start-up activities differ from the management of an existing business. This point is also emphasised by Brown (2000) as entrepreneurship further consists of creativity, innovation and risk taking. Gibb (1983) summarised and illustrated the differences between business education and entrepreneurship education (see table 2).[4]

This dissertation has a more general understanding of the objectives of entrepreneurship education which follows Garavan and O'Cinneide (1994a) and Jacob et al. (2003). Garavan and O'Cinneide (1994a) pointed on the basis of their study out that...

- the acquisition of germane knowledge to entrepreneurship,

- the acquisition of skills in the techniques, the analysis of business situation and the composition of action plans,

- the identification and stimulation of entrepreneurial drive, skills and talent,

- the development of attitudes toward change, the encouragement of new start-ups and other entrepreneurial ventures,

---

[4] Gibb (1983) did not differ between entrepreneurship education and training. Hynes (1996) argues, however, that entrepreneurship education and training can not be used as synonyms and have to be distinguished. She sees entrepreneurship education as prerequisite of training. Entrepreneurship education teaches fundamental or necessary basic abilities and skills. Entrepreneurship training, in contrast, describes a more systematic and planned effort to change or develop skills, knowledge etc. through learning experience. Within this paper no differentiation will be done, as the prevailing opinion in scientific literature uses both phrases mainly in combination with each other.

Table 2: Effect of focus on the process and utilisation of learning

University/business school	Entrepreneurial
Critical judgement after analysis of large amount of information	"Gut feel" decision making with limited information
Understanding and recalling the information itself	Understanding the values of those who transmit and filter information
Assuming goals away	Recognising the wildly varied goals of others
Seeking (impersonally) to verify absolute truth by study of information	Making decisions on the basis of judgement of trust and competence of people
Understanding basic principles of society in the metaphysical sense	Seeking to apply and adjust in practice to basic principles of society
Seeking the correct answer with time to do it	Developing the most appropriate solution under pressure
Learning in the classroom	Learning while and through doing
Gleaning information from experts and authoritative sources	Gleaning information personally from any and everywhere, and weighing it
Evaluation through written assessments	Evaluation by judgement of people and events through direct feedback
Success in learning measured by knowledge-based examination pass	Success in learning by solving problems and learning from failure

Source: Gibb (1987), p. 18.

- the undo of the risk-adverse bias of many analytical techniques,

- the development of support and empathy for all unique aspects of entrepreneurship and

- the creation of an (university-wide) entrepreneurial culture and climate

are objectives for entrepreneurship education. Jacob et al. (2003) noted that especially the creation of an entrepreneurial culture and climate illustrates an objective. Hence, an objective of entrepreneurship education is that not only students,
who are attending entrepreneurship classes, are influenced by entrepreneurship
education efforts, but that a general culture and climate is developed at universities that has the ability to create awareness and change attitudes towards entrepreneurship among students, academics and professors.

2.5.2.4 Content of Entrepreneurship Education

The multitude of different understandings, objectives and the multi-faceted influence of macro-environmental institutions and organisations has led to the development of a heterogeneous design of entrepreneurship education practice at universities. Matlay and Carey (2007) conducted a study with 40 participating universities in the UK and found that almost every university had its own understanding and programme of entrepreneurship education. This heterogeneity can
also be found at German universities (Schmude and Uebelacker, 2001, 2003,
2005).

Solomon et al. (2002) conducted a comprehensive empirical analysis on the content of entrepreneurship education. Therein, they found that skill-building
courses in leadership, new product development, idea generation, negotiation and
the examination of technological innovation should be included (Garavan &
O'Cinneide, 1994; Vesper & McMullan, 1988; McMullan & Long, 1987). Further important areas were sources of venture capital (Zeithaml & Rice, 1987;
Vesper & McMullan, 1988), ambiguity tolerance (Ronstadt, 1987), entrepreneur
as career (Hills, 1988; Donckels, 1991), characteristics of the entrepreneurial personality (Hills, 1988; Scott & Twomey, 1998; Hood & Young, 1993), and idea
protection (Vesper & McMullan, 1988). In addition, Pleschak and Welsch (1990)
draw, attention to the combination of the disciplinary structure of courses and the
evolutionary business development process. Vesper and McMullan (1988) point
out that classical or core functional areas also have to be included (e.g. marketing, accounting, finance, taxes etc.), however with a specific focus on the needs
of business start-ups.

The empirical analysis of Solomon et al. (2002) further showed which types of
learning tools were used in the field of entrepreneurship pedagogy. A common

tool is the business plan seminar which was reported by e.g. Garavan and O'Cinneide (1994), Gartner and Vesper (1994), Hills (1988) and Vesper and McMullan (1988). Behavioural (Stumpf et al., 1991) and computer simulations were also reported (Brawer, 1997). Field trips and the use of video films (Klatt, 1988), also belonged as well to the tools as computer simulations (Brawer, 1997) and consultation with entrepreneurs (Solomon et al., 1994). A similar catalogue was presented by Voigt et al. (2006). Vance (1991) adds to this catalogue that storytelling should be a formalised part of entrepreneurship education tools.

To classify the spectrum of existing approaches Pleschka and Welsch (1990) offer two frameworks. The first framework combines the two dimensions degree of integration and number of courses and degree of integration. The entrepreneurship education can reach from a single course that is not supported and not linked with other established curricula to the integrated programme. The integrated programme is characterised by a full complement of coordinated courses and a complete integration into the curriculum. In addition, bonds have been forged to external institutions and organisations (see figure 10).

Figure 10: Designs of entrepreneurship education

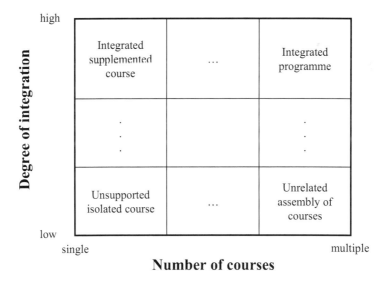

Source: Pleschka and Welsch (1990), p. 63.

The second framework incorporates the stages of transition with the number of disciplines. The first dimension focuses on problems, deficiencies and crises that occur during the business development. The second dimension covers the study areas that could be necessary and helpful to solve these challenges. As the problems increase in number and complexity over time the inclusion of different disciplines is required (see figure 11).

Figure 11: Requirements on entrepreneurship education in the business development

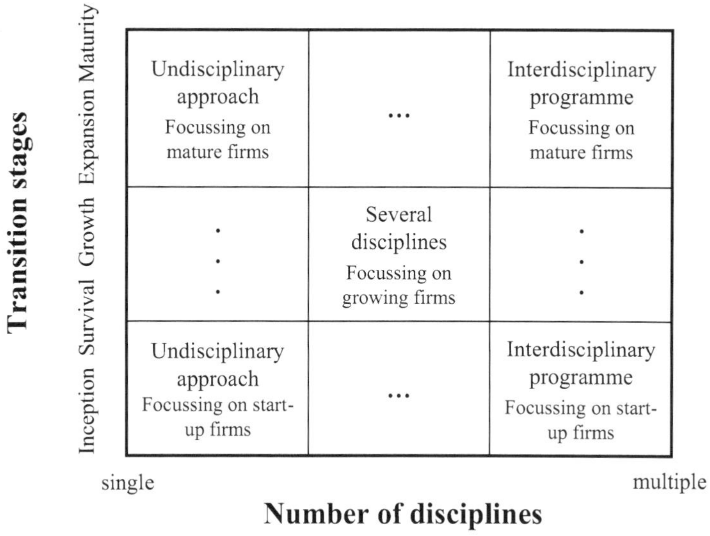
Transition stages
Inception Survival Growth Expansion Maturity
Undisciplinary approach
Focussing on mature firms
...
Interdisciplinary programme
Focussing on mature firms
Several disciplines
Focussing on growing firms
Undisciplinary approach
Focussing on start-up firms
...
Interdisciplinary programme
Focussing on start-up firms
single
multiple
Number of disciplines

Source: Pleschka and Welsch (1990), p. 65.

2.5.3 Organisational Socialisation Strategies and Entrepreneurship Education

To achieve the intended effect on students, organisational socialisation strategies and tactics are used in the entrepreneurship education. In this context, Van Maanen (1978) identified seven major strategies which can be used by organisations to exert influence on their members:

- Collective vs. individual socialisation processes

- Formal vs. informal socialisation processes

- Sequential vs. non-sequential steps in socialisation processes

- Fixed vs. variable socialisation processes

- Serial vs. disjunctive socialisation processes

- Tournament vs. contest socialisation processes

- Investiture vs. divestiture socialisation processes

The first strategy indicates whether people perceive something in a group or as an individual. In the collective socialisation process individuals are put together to a group and share a common set of experiences. When individuals perceive a socialisation programme in a collective, the feelings, thoughts and actions of the group members almost always show "in the same boat" consciousness. Business plan seminars and business simulations illustrate tools of collective socialisation in the entrepreneurship education, as problems have to be solved and goals have to be achieved in a group. Individual socialisation processes focuses solely on the individual. Individuals make experiences alone and almost in isolation from each other (Van Maanen, 1977). Examples for an individual socialisation process in entrepreneurship education are obligatory internships in business start-ups.

The formality of a socialisation process constitutes the second strategy. It describes the degree to which the setting for socialisation is segregated from the organisational context and to which the role as a newcomer is stressed out (Van Maanen, 1978). Formal socialisation sees a complete segregation while informal socialisation occurs in the normal organisational context. Entrepreneurship education mainly occurs as informal socialisation. Lectures and seminars of entrepreneurship education are mainly embedded in the regular curriculum of disciplines. The socialisation is, hence, neither completely segregated nor is the role as beginner emphasised.

Sequential socialisation strategy highlights the transitional process. The socialisation can be characterised by discrete identifiable steps or steps which are unknown, continually changing and/or non-specific. Depending on the entrepreneurship programme, both strategies can be found in practice. In the classification of Pleschak and Welsch (1990) the first would correspond to an integrated programme that is studied in successive order while the latter would be unsupported isolated course(s).

Fixed and variable socialisation processes are related to the temporary transition. In contrast to fixed socialisation processes, variable socialisation processes possess no standardised transition. University study is in general seen as a fixed process (Van Maanen, 1978). However, if the entrepreneurship education programme is not constructed in a successive progression, the transition can become partly variable.

Another kind of strategy is the serial or disjunctive socialisation process. In a serial socialisation process experienced members of an organisation act as mentors for beginners (Van Maanen, 1977). If new members do not have such an orientation it is called a disjunctive socialisation process. In universities a more serial socialisation strategy can be found since informal experience exchanges between students from different semesters can be assumed.

The strategy of tournament or contest socialisation process refers to the distinction between superiors and inferiors in the same rank and the resulting, possible access to specific socialisation programmes (Van Maanen, 1978). Normally, it can be assumed that entrepreneurship education applies to a contest socialisation as the attendance of lectures and seminars is mainly not linked to abilities, background and/or ambition or a selection process. This fact has been criticised by Raichaudhuri (2005) who stated that it is necessary to select the attendees of entrepreneurship education.

The last strategy is linked to investiture and divestiture socialisation processes. The strategy concerns the degree to which the socialisation process disconfirms or confirms the usefulness and viability of existing personal characteristics (Van Maanen, 1977). In contrast to investiture processes, divestiture processes are targeted to change the personality of members. In entrepreneurship, a mixture of investiture and divestiture socialisation processes can be found. Through entrepreneurship education for example, the self-efficacy shall be promoted (Cox, 1996), ambiguity tolerance skills and attitudes taught (Ronstadt, 1987).

2.5.4 Organisational Socialisation and Entrepreneurship Education in the Theoretical Framework

Due to different understandings, definitions and objectives of different entrepreneurship programmes have been developed. As a consequence not just one successful concept of entrepreneurship education, especially at universities can be identified as a role concept (Matlay, 2006). This fact has contributed to a debate about the effectiveness of entrepreneurship education. This debate, however, has been decided for the proponents of entrepreneurship education. Kuratko (2003) emphasises in this context: "It is becoming clear that entrepreneurship, or certain facets of it, can be taught. Business educators and professionals have evolved beyond the myth that entrepreneurs are born, not made." (p. 10). Several studies have proved the positive effect of entrepreneurship education. Clark et al. (1984) came in their study to the conclusion that a relationship exists between new venture creation and entrepreneurial education. Peterman and Kennedy (2003) found in their study that entrepreneurship education increased the perception of desirability and feasibility towards starting a business. A study by Voigt et al. (2006) at the University of Erlangen-Nuremberg showed that entrepreneurship education has a significant influence on the entrepreneurial behaviour of students. The results of Alain et al. (2006) strongly suggest that entrepreneurship education has a strong effect for some students.

Hence, organisational socialisation in the form of entrepreneurship education can have at least an influence on the entrepreneurial attitude or determinants of intention. Through the organisational socialisation process are, furthermore, commonsensical beliefs, principles, norms and attitudes transferred onto the student. By teaching essential aspects of entrepreneurship self-efficacy, respectively perceived behavioural control, can be increased as the confidence in the ability to perform entrepreneurial behaviour is strengthened. The influence is exerted either directly via the lectures, seminars and courses or through created entrepreneurial culture and climate in an organisation. This created climate and culture further promotes awareness and change attitudes towards entrepreneurship among students that have not attended entrepreneurship education lectures, seminars and courses.

The theory of planned behaviour (Ajzen, 1991) has pointed out that attitude is a reliable factor for predicting intention which has been confirmed by several authors (e.g. Douglas & Shepard, 2002; Bagozzi et al., 1989). It can be argued that entrepreneurship education influences the development of a higher intention to start a business directly or indirectly. Entrepreneurship education as form of organisational socialisation illustrates, therewith, a fundamental determinant of entrepreneurship (especially academic entrepreneurship). Simultaneously, it has to be bore in mind that entrepreneurship education addresses an individual that is shaped or affected not only by the socialisation efforts of the organisations but also by social learning processes (e.g. rooted in family background). Figure 12 includes entrepreneurship education as form of organisational socialisation into the theoretical framework. Correlations between the social learning and organisational socialisation are not displayed.

Figure 12: Entrepreneurship education in the theoretical framework

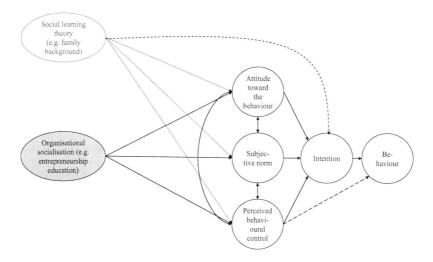

2.6   Gender and Gender Theory

2.6.1   Sex and Gender

Following the prevailing opinion in social and behavioural sciences gender and sex do not describe the same aspect (Verheul, 2005). Sex focuses on the biological aspect, respectively the physiological differences between men and women. The biological determinism uses sex as a reason to explain differences between

men and women, as those differences can be solely attributed to a different biological precondition. Existing social arrangements between women and men are,
hence, unavoidable. Supporters of the determinism assume, that inherited, inborn
biological differences are responsible for the development of the personality, social behaviour and intelligence of a person. Sex-specific inequalities are explained by the different genes (Verheul, 2005). According to the prevailing opinion in scientific literature, biological differences are however not sufficient to
explain completely the different position and status of men and women in the
society (Voigt, 1994).

Gender, in contrast, combines biological sex with the paradigm of the different
socialisation to explain recognisable differences (Korabik, 1999). Socialisation
comprises the communicative process, in which individuals learn and further develop the rules and culture of their society (Newman, 1995). Socialisation is,
therewith, an ongoing process, intertwined with the socio-political development
(Hoerning, 2000). Social experiences, social attribution and informal learning
processes, that usually occur from the moment of birth, influence the development of gender. Supporters of the different socialisation argue that an individual
learns what it means to be a woman or a man and how to behave in an appropriate way as a result of the responses of parents and the social environment to
his/her sex. In the same sex different experiences can be made during the socialisation process and the social gender can be different from the biological sex
(Fischer et al., 1993; Verheul, 2005; Becker-Schmidt, 1993). Figure 13 illustrates
the correlation between sex and gender.

Figure 13: Components of gender

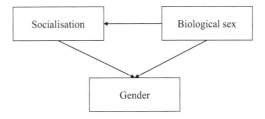

2.6.2 Gender in Entrepreneurship Research

In entrepreneurship research a growing number of publications have laid the focus on gender, since Eleonore Schwartz's article was published in 1976 in a no-

table academic journal. On a worldwide scale, scholars have examined the meaning of gender in the context of entrepreneurship across a wide range of topics (Greene et al., 2003).

Regarding the industry choice of female and male entrepreneurs Watkins and Watkins (1986) found that a lack of prior working experience would influence the choice of industry for the business foundation and women would thus prefer to found in traditional female-dominated sectors. Verheul and Thurik (2001) could confirm these results in their study with 2000 Dutch entrepreneurs in which female entrepreneurs were more likely to have founded in the service sector. Also the studies of Hisrich and Brush (1984), Sexton and Smilor (1986), Hisrich and O'Brien (1981) have shown that women are more likely to found in traditional, female-dominated industries (retail and service).

The performance and success of female- and male-owned businesses represents a topic in which a heated academic debate can be found. On the one side, it is argued that female-owned businesses are less successful than male's (Wojahn, 1986). Fisher et al. (1993) found that men's business consistently outperformed women's. Male-owned businesses had more employees, a higher annual income and higher annual sales. The income, in addition, grew faster than women's and men's enterprises had higher levels of sales per employee. However, no difference was found regarding the return. On the other side Kalleberg and Leicht (1991) pointed out that businesses founded by women were not more likely to go bankrupt or to be less successful. Johnson and Storey (1993) came in their longitudinal study to the conclusion that female-owned businesses had created more stable enterprises than the enterprises of their male counterparts, but that the turnover for male-owned businesses was higher. The debate of performance and success is also linked to the debate whether appropriate measures are used to evaluate and compare female- and male-owned businesses. Authors like Lewis (2006) argued that the methods of measurements would be gender biased and subsequently not appropriate. Carter et al. (2001) pointed to the fact that a different motivational background could illustrate the basis for different outcomes.

To the general motivation for becoming an entrepreneur a multitude of articles were published (e.g. Ljunggren & Kolvereid, 1996; Romano, 1994; Dhaliwal, 1998; Fisher et al., 1993, Hisrich & Öztürk, 1999, Rosa & Dawson, 2006). Moult and Anderson (2005) categorised motivation into push and pull factors. While pull-factors are associated with choice, push-factors emphasise the necessity for entrepreneurial behaviour. Need for achievement (e.g. Rosa & Dawson, 2006, Hisrich & Öztürk, 1999) and job satisfaction (e.g. Hisrich & Öztürk, 1999) illustrate pull-factors, while economic necessity (e.g. Lerner et al. 1997; Hisrich & Öztürk 1999) and avoiding discrimination (e.g. Dhaliwal 1998) are push factors. Romano (1994) examined among other variables in this context the perception of success. She found that men and women believed that money is an important component of entrepreneurial success. However, while men defined success in terms of achieving a goal, women saw success as having control over their destinies, doing something fulfilling and building ongoing relationships with clients. Similar results were found by Ljunggren and Kolvereid, (1996). Fischer et al. (1993) had contradicting results. In their study women had a greater motivation than men. In general, it is however, argued that men and women are motivated by similar factors (Moult & Anderson, 2005; Birley, 1989).

The entrepreneurial network was examined from two perspectives. The first perspective highlights how female and male entrepreneurs build and establish their network. In this context Buttner (1993) stated that men and women have different priorities. "Men's motivation are often more 'instrumental' (seeking personal gain), while women have more 'affective' considerations in social relationships. As a result of socialisation, women may have more difficulty than men in putting personal feelings aside in business relationships" (p. 62). The second perspective focuses on the access to entrepreneurial networks. Therein, a gender-related disadvantage for women was identified. Buttner (1993) argued that it has always been difficult to enter "old boy networks". Aldrich (1989) pointed out that the network of men included just a few women, while men were more easily included into the network of women.

Next to the access to entrepreneurial networks, financing and acquisition of capital are used as an example to illustrate that female entrepreneurs are confronted with obstacles and discrimination (Buttner, 1993). Buttner and Rosen (1988, 1989) examined with an experimental design, whether women have to cope to a higher extent with obstacles in getting bank loans. Their first paper showed that men were always rated closer to successful entrepreneurs than women. Within the second paper, however, no evidence could be found that stereotypes influenced the funding decision. Women even got higher counteroffers than men, when the business plan had been read. Carter and Rosa (1998) laid their research

focus on the financing of male- and female-owned business and found two differences. Within their study men used larger amounts of money of capital than
women to start their business. Furthermore, gender differences could be identified in financial arrangements. Men used institutional finance (e.g. bank loans) to
a higher degree.

Also the education and human capital was examined through the gender lens.
Watkins and Watkins (1986) found that women differ from men in working experience and background. Women were less likely to have prior work experience.
Fischer et al. (1993) reached to similar conclusions. In their study women had
less experience than man in working in similar firms, managing employees and
helping to start other businesses. Based on a study of Australian business owners
Barret (1995) suggested that female entrepreneurs have less access to some kinds
of experience and correspondingly they value more the one which they can access. In addition, it was easier for men to enter mainly female-dominated industries than it was for women in male-dominated businesses. DeTienne and Chandler (2007) looked at the difference of opportunity identification regarding the
usage of human capital and tried to explore gender differences. They concluded
that men and women are similar in using their existing individual stock of human
capital to identify opportunities. However, fundamental differences in the process
were recognized. Inferences on the innovativeness could, however, not be made.

The importance of social roles has also been examined. In particular, the work-
life-balance has been analysed in this context. The accommodation of work and
childrearing and the inherent link to work-family balance was found more important for women than for men (e.g. Cromie, 1987; Buttner, 1993; Chu, 2000). On
basis of a literature review, Moult and Anderson (2005) came to the conclusion
that female entrepreneurs differ from their male counterparts stating that even "if
all else is equal in terms of motivation, there is evidence that family, and pre-
sumably family responsibility, plays a larger role, vis-à-vis business, for women
than for men" (p.260). Carter et al. (1997) examined whether performance differences can be explained by variations of initial founding strategies and resources.
Therein, they analysed whether women have fewer resources for their start-up
and whether they would try to overcome those shortcomings through a founding
strategy. Strategic choice is therein seen as a result of socialisation experiences in
which females and males fundamentally differ. Carter et al. (1997) found that
women owners used founding strategies to reduce the odds of discontinuing

business, had fewer start-up resources and smaller businesses at the beginning. They concluded that the findings were probably a conservative representation of gender-related situational disadvantages.

Research has also been conducted to examine the effect of gender on the career choice. Therefore, Bandura's concept of self-efficacy (1977) was combined with the social learning theory (Bandura, 1968, 1977). Scherer et al. (1990) stated that males and females have in general approximately the same level of self-efficacy for careers that are dominated by their gender. In the context of entrepreneurship, women have been reported to have less self-efficacy than men (Birley, 1989). Scherer et al. (1990) confirmed this in their empirical study. Barret (1995) added that men were more likely to enter a female-dominated industry than women. Kourilsky and Walstad (1998) used a sample of the Gallup Organization with a sample of approximately 1000 male and female youths. Both males and females showed a low level of entrepreneurship knowledge, but females were more aware of their deficiencies in this context than their male counterparts. Simultaneously, the probability in the female sub sample was lower to start a business. Hence, their self-efficacy or perceived behavioural control could have influenced negatively the intention to start a business. Bosma et al. (2008) have indicated that in high-income countries, men are about twice as likely as women to be involved in early-stage entrepreneurial activity. For countries Central Asia and in Eastern Europe the gender gap was even bigger: men were 2.3 times as likely to be early-stage entrepreneurs as women. Thus, it could be argued that, outside their families, women have less entrepreneurial role-models that could positively influence the career decision.

2.6.3 Gender in the Theoretical Framework

As the literature review has shown gender is a fundamental influence on all aspects of entrepreneurship like the way a business is founded, what kind of industry is chosen, the decision to launch smaller or bigger, to found in a team or alone, the establishment of an network etc. Gender is a result of biological sex in combination with a different socialisation. The socialisation process starts with the birth and influences an individual from earliest moment of life due to the reaction of the social environment. Hence, its outstanding position is rooted in the fact that it influences all learning experiences (Kolip, 1999) and, subsequently, attitudes and subjective norms. The gender-related socialisation shapes and affects directly the personality. Regarding for example the motivation a conservative, traditional understanding of social roles is mirrored as it was found that women tend to take the balance of work and family more into consideration than men. Even differences between the gender were found referring to the level of self-efficacy respectively perceived behavioural control in the context of the theory of planned behaviour. As women perceive their behavioural control more negative than men their intention decreases and so does the likelihood to develop entrepreneurial behaviour. Figure 14 includes gender into the theoretical framework. Correlations between the social learning and organisational socialisation are not displayed.

Figure 14: Subsumption of gender perspective in the theoretical framework

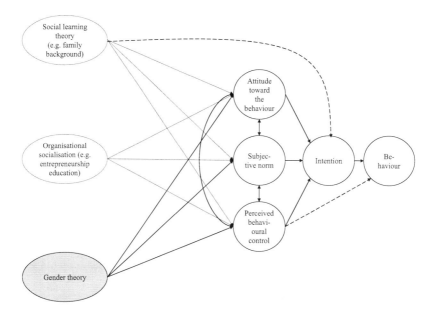

2.7   Linkages to the Chapters

The previous chapters have shown that social learning theory, organisational socialisation and gender illustrate fundamental influences on the process from intention to entrepreneurial behaviour. Accordingly, those factors are fundamental determinants of entrepreneurial behaviour respectively entrepreneurship.

Matthews and Moser (1996) argued that it is essential for understanding "how interest in small firm ownership unfolds, it would be best to attempt to study it before the decision is made to open a business. These processes are best studied prospectively and over time" (p. 32). Woodier (2007) further states that "intentions could slowly change over time and that the longer the time period between intention and behaviour; the greater chance unforeseen events will produce changes in intentions. However only few exceptions in the entrepreneurship literature (e.g. Matthews & Moser, 1996; Shaver et al., 1996) can be found which have a longitudinal character. Within chapter two the effect of social learning (family background) and specific cognitions related to the perceived behavioural control in form of fostering and hindering perceptions towards self-employment are examined. Attention is also given to gender similarities or differences and to catching a glimpse of entrepreneurial related variables as they occur over time. The panel results will be compared with a cross-sectional cohort study. In the university surveyed no entrepreneurship-related lectures, courses or seminars are included into the study curriculum until the fifth semester. As the surveys were conducted in the first and third semester the influence of the entrepreneurship programme is only indirectly through the established entrepreneurship culture.

A longitudinal panel approach in combination with a cross-sectional cohort study was also applied in chapter two to look at gender related differences regarding the motivation and goals that influence the entrepreneurial intention. Special attention will be paid to three different aspects. First, the goals that illustrate the system of objectives pursued in the working life by women and men will be analysed. Hence, attitudes towards entrepreneurial behaviour can be unfolded. Second, the perception of fostering factors towards a business foundation will be analysed which can give indications about the level of self-efficacy or respectively perceived behaviour control among males and females. Third, an analysis will be conducted of how women and men perceive the success of a newly founded company in general and the success of their own (potential) company in particular. As the surveys were conducted in the first and third semester, the results offer hints as to how the educational programme influences male and female students. Entrepreneurship education programme, however, affect the students only indirectly through the created entrepreneurial culture

The fourth chapter concentrates on a later point in time as students chosen in the survey sample are in average in the fifth semester and are subsequently in majority in a graduate equivalent period of study. The entrepreneurship education programme established at the surveyed university influences the students not only indirectly over the created entrepreneurship culture but also through entrepreneurship lectures, seminars and courses that are included into the regular curriculum. In addition, entrepreneurship and business start-up can be chosen after entering the graduate level which increases the possible influence. The goal of this study is to cover a variety of influences on founding intention (family background, educational environment, and cognition) analysed in regard to gender.

Pittaway and Cope (2007) indicated that entrepreneurship education programmes differ in reality within different countries as a consequence of different higher education systems. However, in some cases conclusions were drawn for entrepreneurship education as a whole. Pittaway and Cope (2007) point, therefore, at the need for more international, comparative studies. Within the fifth chapter a comparison of different education programmes in different countries is conducted. Therein a comparison between UK and German students is carried out that examines similarities and differences in the determinants of intention and intention itself. The findings can help to uncover cultural differences and illustrate a starting point for the identification of best practices in entrepreneurship education.

Figure 15 summarises the conducted surveys with students as survey sample along the procedure of the study programme. For the longitudinal studies of chapter one and two surveys were conducted in semester one and three.

Figure 15: Surveys conducted for chapter 1 – 4 in the curriculum

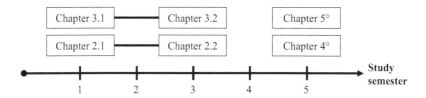

° Average student in his fifth semester

The theory of planned behaviour is rooted in the theory of reasoned action that states that the likelihood to show entrepreneurial behaviour increases with the belief that the performance of a particular behaviour will lead to a specific outcome (Madden et al., 1992). In the context of entrepreneurship this means that entrepreneurial behaviour leads to the establishment of a successful enterprise. The theory of planned behaviour argues that the probability for actual behaviour is related to the extent to which an individual intends to perform this behaviour and perceives his/hers behavioural control (Ajzen, 1991). The perceived behavioural control indicates the level to which an individual believes to have the necessary resources and opportunities. An external factor that can influence the perception of behavioural control and can improve the likelihood of survival and success of a business start up is the existence of a sophisticatedly developed support organisation infrastructure. Therefore, the support organisation infrastructure of Germany will be analysed in chapter six.

Figure 16: Classification of chapters in the theoretical framework

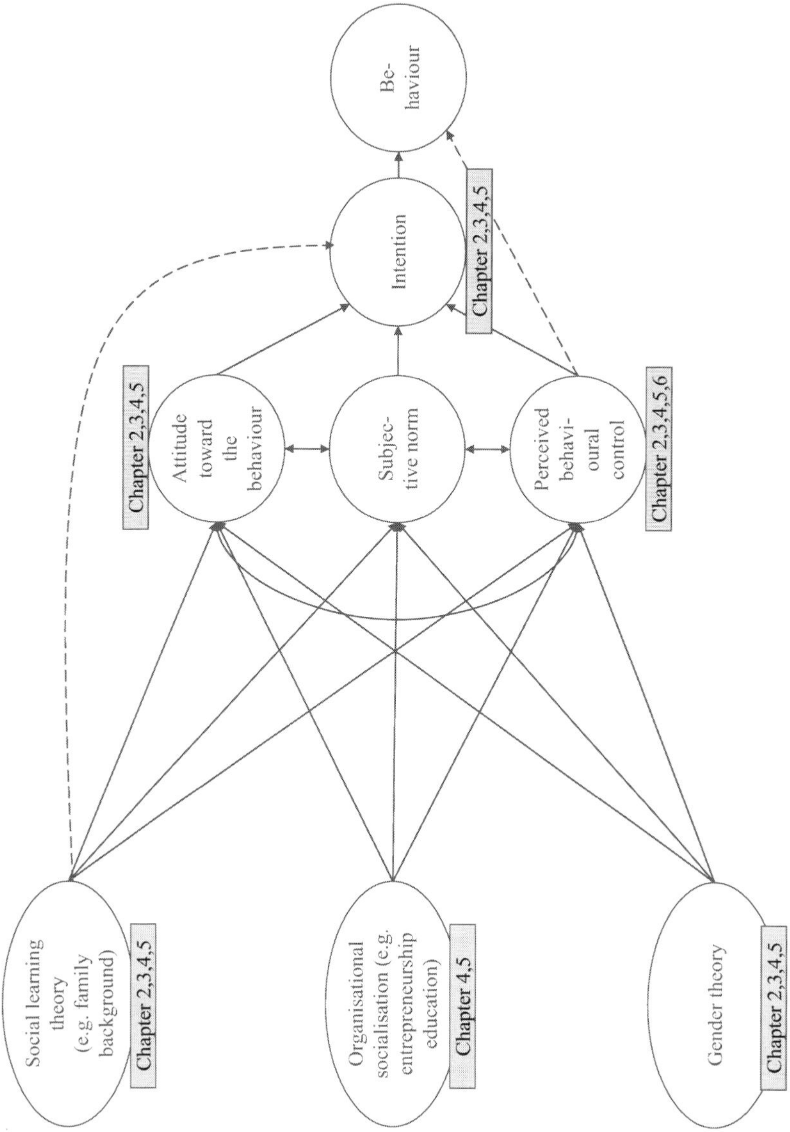

3   Gender-related Differences in the Founding Intention

3.1   Introduction

Whereas in the recent past entrepreneurship education is flourishing (Hisrich, 2006), the global entrepreneurship monitor reports that youth entrepreneurship has not enjoyed similar growth.. For example, in 2006 the percentage of start-ups founded by young people sunk in comparison to 2005. And youth entrepreneurship still remains only a minor part of entrepreneurship research and most of literature on the topic focuses on entrepreneurs after the commencement of their business activities - that is during the start-up or the later phases of corporate development. Potential entrepreneurs and the pre-start-up phase seem to be neglected or, at least, they have not attracted the corresponding attention yet. However, there are several models which deal with a corporate life cycle, but it is quite surprising that most of the models begin with the start-up phase and go on to the early development phase, but very few include the pre-start-up phase as a separate stage of the corporate development

Understanding the consequences of intentions - particularly actions- requires that the antecedents of intention.are understood (Krueger et al., 2000). Following Bagozzi et al. (1989), intentions are the best predictors for planned behaviour. Hence, "understanding and predicting new venture initiation requires research using theory-driven models that adequately reflect the complex perception-based processes underlying intentional, planned behaviours such as new venture initiation." (Krueger & Carsrud, 1993, p. 315). The most common approach in this area is from Ajzen (1991), developed in the context of social psychology. This theory identifies three general antecedents of intention: attitude towards behaviour, subjective norms and perceived feasibility. In this study, special attention is paid to motives, perceived hurdles and family background as antecedents of the founding intention of students. Intention, however, is not activity; therefore, results from several surveys will be presented, in order to see if the intention has become activity and to track down possible changes over time. Further, all of these aspects will be researched under the gender lense, as former scientific literature has found several differences. In general scholars like Fischer et al. (1993) have suggested the use of feminism approaches as theoretical background. They argue that the perspectives of liberal and social feminism can help in understanding the nature and implication of issues related to gender in the context of entrepreneurship. Hence, the social feminism perspective (rooted from social learning theory to psychoanalysis) will be used as theoretical background for this dissertation. It argues that men and women are fundamentally the same, but differ in their points of view due to different experiences from the earliest moments of life. However, it scientists continue to debate whether gender differences truly exist and, if yes, in which areas and to what extent.

According to the global entrepreneurship monitor (Sternberg & Lückgen, 2005) and the KfW Start-up Monitor 2005 (Hofmann et al., 2005), in Germany fewer women than men are interested in founding their own company (only 29%), although women represent half of the employed population. Over the last twenty years, academics and economic organisations have demonstrated a growing interest in women entrepreneurs, especially in the United States and Canada where the number of women that owned businesses has been rising. Female entrepreneurship is now considered to be an important sources of growth, employment, and innovation. In the United States, women-owned businesses are the fastest growing sector of all new ventures (Becker-Blease & Sohl, 2007). However, very little is known about women entrepreneurs (Orhan, 2001) and less is known about potential female entrepreneurs and above all female students.

3.2   Literature Review

3.2.1 Gender

In the past twenty years, the field of female entrepreneurship, and in extension, gender similarities or differences in the founding behaviour have attracted a lot of attention (e.g. Walker & Joyner, 1999; Mueller, 2004; Birley, 1989), even if the focus was placed upon existing instead of potential entrepreneurs.

A literature review conducted by Brush in 1992 revealed that male and female entrepreneurs have more similarities than differences in individual characteristics. Regarding the reasons for becoming self-employed several motivation variables like independence (Cromie, 1987), avoiding low paid occupation, escaping supervision and the constraint of subservient roles (Goffee & Scase, 1985) were identified. As far as venture performance is concerned, Kalleberg and Leicht (1991) found that businesses founded by women were not more likely to go bankrupt or to be less successful. In the literature, however, some gender-related differences could be found as well. According to the global entrepreneurship monitor executive report of 2007 (Bosma et al., 2008), men, in general, are more active in entrepreneurship than women. Furthermore, female and male entrepreneurs differ with respect to their personal and business profile (Hisrich & O'Brien, 1982; Fischer et al., 1993; Chaganti & Parasuraman, 1996; Carter et al., 1997; Verheul, 2003), the fear of failure is more dominant to women as to men (Sternberg et al., 2004) and women are more likely to stress personal expectancies while men are more likely to stress economic expectancies during the start-up process of a firm (Ljunggren & Kolvereid, 1996).

Studies on potential entrepreneurs that have taken into consideration among other factors also the gender factor include the following: Wang and Wong's study (2004) on university undergraduate students in Singapore, Matthew's and Moser's study (1996) on business graduates in the US, Singh and DeNoble's study on students from a state university in the US, Kourilsky's and Walstad's study (1998) on high school students in the US. The results of these studies are presented in the following sections.

3.2.2 Business Foundation Intention

A very common way to describe the development of a company is the use of corporate life cycles, which vary from two stages (Dodge et al., 1994) to ten stages (Adizes, 1999). Most of these models begin with the start-up phase and go on to the early development phase, the very early phases of the business foundation process, especially the opportunity recognition process, are often neglected. Hence, the pre-start-up phase has not attracted the necessary attention yet, as particularly in this phase, factors like personal intentions, motivation and family background etc. play the most important role in the final employment status choice. In this context, research shows that the intention to start a company is central to entrepreneurship (Bird, 1988; Krueger, 1993). Discovering founding intentions is important, because the opportunity identification process is clearly an intentional process and it is a central element within entrepreneurship education to explain and predict entrepreneurial activities (Krueger et al., 2000). In this context, Krueger et al. (2000) argue further that promoting entrepreneurial intentions means to promote public perceptions of feasibility and desirability. Moreover, Ljunggren and Kolvereid (1996) state that researching the reasons for gender differences in entrepreneurial intentions will support the understanding of the lower entrepreneurial activity of women compared to men.

Within the plethora of research on entrepreneurship, there is not enough research conducted on entrepreneurial intention among students yet. In addition, little is known about gender-specific differences in the pre-start-up phase (Mueller, 2004; Ljunggren & Kolvereid, 1996). This is surprising, as e.g. 16% of boys and girls between the age of 15 and 20 in Germany state that they want to found their own business in future (IDW, 2008). However, Wang and Wong (2004) concentrated on the level and the determinants of interest in entrepreneurship among university students in Singapore and have found among others that whereas students evaluated their business knowledge as poor, their interest to start-up a company is high. Scott and Twomey (1988) focused on university students' career aspiration in three countries (USA, U.K., Ireland), and found that the U.S sample aspiring to self-employment was low (25%) in comparison to the U.K. with 41% and Ireland with 34%. In a survey of 372 Norwegian business graduates (conducted 1996), Kolvereid (1996) found that 38% preferred self-employment. Lüthje and Franke (2003) report that from a sample of 2.193 engineering students, 44% indicate, that they would quite probably and 11% that they would very probably run their own company after the completion of their studies. From the interviewed students only 3% were already self-employed. In general, research indicates that there is a relationship between gender and entrepreneurial intention (Stein & Nurul, 2004). Moreover, according to Kourilsky and Walstad (1998), females are significantly less likely than males (62%-72%) interested to start their own business. Still, there are only a few empirical results yet, which examine change of intention over time. In this context, Woodier (2007) states that "intentions could slowly change over time and that the longer the time period between intention and behaviour; the greater the chance that unforeseen events will produce changes in intentions" (p. 6).

Research question 1: Do male and female students differ in their founding intention?

Research question 2: Do male and female students have a stable intention towards becoming self-employed over time?

3.2.3   The Influence of the Family Background

Singh and DeNoble (2003) showed that personality, gender and having a close self-employed relative altogether have a strong positive impact on the attitude on self-employment. Moreover, Chen et al. (1998) indicated that the number of entrepreneurial friends and relatives was positive in respect of entrepreneurial decision. Regarding the family background, Klandt (1984) found in his study that the father's profession has an effect on the occupational decision of the son and the daughter, while the mother's influence is mostly limited to the daughter. Therefore, the father's profession seems to have a more universal influence. According to DeMartino and Barbato (2003) especially women are more influenced by the family background to found a business than men. However, particularly male students expressed a stronger intention toward becoming an entrepreneur than female students did (Chen et al., 1998). An explanation for the influence of family background offers Kolvereid (1996), who states that family background, gender, and self-employment experience only indirectly influence intentions to become self-employed through their effect on attitude, subjective norm and perceived behavioural control. Hence, there is some evidence, that the business family background strongly supports the children's propensity to take up an entrepreneurial career (Scott & Twomey, 1988; Römer-Paakkanen & Rauhala, 2007; Wang & Wong, 2004; Benett & Dann, 2000).

Research question 3: Do male and female students differ towards becoming self-employed in regard to their family background?

3.2.4   Cognition towards Entrepreneurship (Motives and Hurdles)

Research shows that the educational level in general does not fully explain the intention to become an entrepreneur (Reynolds, 2007). As far as potential entrepreneurs (students) are concerned, Heinemann and Welter (2007) found that motives that did not have to do with money (e.g. implementation of own ideas, freedom of decision and of handling, self realisation) were more important for students than money based motives. Lack of equity, high risk and high level of bureaucracy have been seen as hindering factors (Heinemann & Welter, 2007). Möller (1998) found that the important founding reservations were the lack of start-up finance and the high degree of risk. Especially students with a low intention to start an own business saw those reasons as hindering factors. Furthermore, "Too much work and too little spare time" was named as an important hindering factor.

Most of the studies that examine potential entrepreneurs that deal with motives and hurdles have not analysed the influence of gender yet. However, bearing in mind the basic assumption of the social feminism (Fischer et al., 1993), that women differ fundamentally from men due to their socialisation, it is necessary to analyse how gender affects the influence of inhibiting and fostering factors on the founding intention. Therefore, the influence of cognition on the founding intention through the gender-lens will be investigated. In the literature of existing entrepreneurs, more similarities than differences in the motivation of the two gender have been identified (e.g. Birley, 1989). For example, researchers found that independence is a strong motivator for both males and females (Cromie, 1987; Shane et al., 1991) and that is valid also for achievement and status (Cromie, 1987). However, gender differences were found in the motivation of male and female entrepreneurs. Women are less likely than male entrepreneurs to be motivated by advancement, but rather by family and lifestyle (DeMartino & Barbato, 2003). Financial gain was found a strong motivation for males in general and less for women (Bradley & Boles, 2003). As far as hurdles are concerned, the availability of equity capital for women entrepreneurs is usually lower because for example they were not paid as high as men in earlier jobs (Verheul & Thurik, 2001). Drawing from the literature of existing entrepreneurs, one could argue that there are only small differences in the motivation and the perceived hurdles among male and female students. The following research questions are posed:

Research question 4: Do male and female students differ in their motivation towards entrepreneurship?

Research question 5: Do male and female students have over time a stable motivation towards becoming self-employed?

Research question 6: Do male and female students differ in their perception of hurdles towards entrepreneurship?

Research question 7: Do male and female students have over time a stable per-ception of hurdles towards becoming self-employed?

Research question 8: Is there an influence of motives toward founding a busi-ness?

Research question 9: Is there an influence of hurdles toward founding a busi-ness?

3.2.5 Longitudinal Studies

Besides a few exceptions in the entrepreneurship literature only a limited number of studies can be found that have a longitudinal character. "In order to better understand how interest in small firm ownership unfolds, it would be best to attempt to study it before the decision is made to open a business. These processes are best studied prospectively and over time." (Matthews & Moser, 1996). In their longitudinal study, Matthews and Moser (1996) found that whereas the interest of males towards self-employment stayed steady over time, females' interest declined. In the literature about (on) existing entrepreneurs, Hisrich and Brush (Greene et al., 2003) conducted one of the first longitudinal studies that had gender as focus. Initial studies were conducted in 1983 and in 1987, they returned to their respondents and found among others that 30-40% of the businesses in the original sample had failed. Furthermore, businesses run by female entrepreneurs showed a revenue increase of about 7% per year. In 1996, their longitudinal study tried to explain the relationship between achievement motivation, locus of control, risk perception and creativity and success at getting into business. One interesting finding is that the difference between innovation and achievement/activity scores was greater among male respondents than among female respondents (Shaver et al., 1996).

3.3   Methodology

3.3.1 Data Collection and Sample Characteristics

Two surveys were conducted between winter term 2006/2007 and winter term 2007/2008 at the University of Erlangen-Nuremberg. In total 553 students par-ticipated in the first and 398 in the second survey. The questionnaires were handed out in lectures that are mainly visited in successive order during the study. For the purpose of this chapter only data from bachelor students will be used who have started their study in the winter term 2006/2007. In general an average responding included student was born 1985 and was studying Business Administration. Following Hakim (2000) the sample fulfils the requirements of a cohort study. The first wave (study I) included 243 students at the start of their study. The proportion of male and female respondents was almost even with 120 men and 122 women. 195 could be allocated in the following survey (study II) to this group. Therefore, the cohort study includes 243, respectively 195 participants for the two waves. From the entire sample 20 male and 38 female respondents could be identified for a panel study (n=58) (see Figure 17).

Figure 17: Data collection and sample characteristics

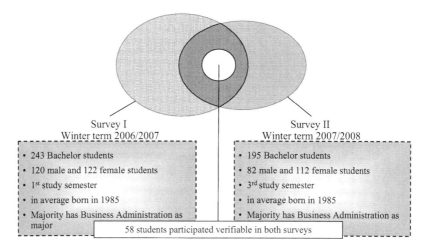

3.3.2 Operationalisation of Variables

Intention

In order to measure entrepreneurial intention, the validated scale by Klandt (1984) was applied. The question used was "Have you personally ever thought about founding your own business?". Possible answers are varying from 1 (=no, not yet), 2 (=yes, occasionally), 3 (=yes, relatively concrete) to 4 (=yes, I have made the decision to become self-employed).

Family Background

To measure the family background of the participants a scale of Möller (1998) was applied. "Manual, skilled or semi-skilled worker", "Salaried professional etc.", "Government employee", "Entrepreneur", "Freelancer or other self-employed" as well as "Other(s)" were given as answer alternatives in order to rate the profession of the parents. The variable family background was dichotomised for father's self-employment (0=not self-employed; 1=self-employed) and mother's self-employment (0=not self-employed; 1=self-employed).

Fostering and Inhibiting Factors

To measure the perception of fostering and inhibiting factors the scale of Möller (1998) was applied. Concerning the fostering factors the question was used "Please indicate which statement would best describe your feelings about starting a business" or respectively for the inhibiting factors "Please indicate which statement would best describe your feelings about NOT starting a business". Answer alternatives reached from 1 (=totally agree) to 5 (=totally disagree) (see table 3).

Table 3: Overview of fostering and inhibiting factors factors

Fostering factors:	Hindering factors:
Self-realisation	Missing business knowledge
Higher independency	Missing concrete business idea
Put studies into action	Missing seed capital
Higher autonomy of decision	Insufficient practical experience
Good economic climate	General missing interest
Realise idea/Pursue own business idea	Missing founding partner /team
	Missing business network
Gain experience	Missing market knowledge
Bear responsibility	Missing market transparency
Higher prestige/social status	Spouse or partnerdisapproves idea
Higher income	High financial risk
Potential profit	Low income
Continue family business	Too much work for too less money
Motivation by friends and family	Too much work and too less spare-time
	Bad economic climate
	Bound to the own company
	Risk of failure
	Missing social appreciation

3.4   Results

In the following chapter at first the descriptive findings will be shown before the statistical results for the panel will be illustrated. Afterwards the results from the cohort study will be presented and the results of both approaches will be compared. Independent t-tests were conducted to find differences between men and women in each survey. Paired t-tests were chosen to identify and analyse changes and development over time (only significant results for the dependent variables will be analysed). In addition, linear regression analyses were conducted for the panel study to examine the effect of motives, hurdles, and family background on founding intention. Different analyses for survey 1 and survey 2 will be presented. Figure 18 and 19 summarise the research framework for the panel and the cohort study.

Figure 18: Research framework (panel)

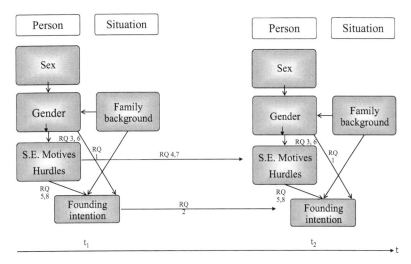

Figure 19: Research framework (cohort study)

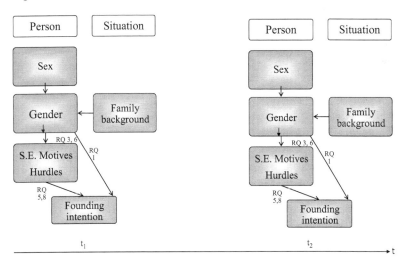

3.4.1 Intention

The descriptive results show that within the panel group and the study cohort the founding intention is quite low. Male and female participants in general have thought only occasionally about founding a business. Regarding the self-employment status of the respondents, only one student in the panel group was already self-employed and the number of self-employed students in the cohort is also small (see table 4).

Table 4: Founding intention, self-employment of parents, own self-employment, study related factors

Founding Intention	Percentage							
	Panel				Study cohort			
	Male		Female		Male		Female	
	2006	2007	2006	2007	2006	2007	2006	2007
No, not yet	36.8	21.1	35.1	18.4	20.4	11.0	35.9	31.5
Yes, occasionally	47.4	52.6	56.8	68.4	46.3	65.8	52.1	61.1
Yes, relatively concrete	5.3	21.1	5.4	7.9	18.5	13.7	7.7	4.6
Yes, I have decided to become self-employed	10.5	5.3	2.7	5.3	14.8	9.6	4.3	2.8
Total	100	100	100	100	100	100	100	100
N	20	20	38	38	108	82	117	12
Self-employment (parents)								
Father	7	6	12	12	20	17	26	34
Mother	3	4	2	1	8	9	11	7
Self-employment (own)								
No.	1	0	1	0	5	2	1	2

As far as gender is concerned the intention to become self-employed is equal within the male and female panel group in each conducted survey both have thought about it occasionally on average. Over time, only women change significantly. Between the first and second survey they have started to think about self-employment to a higher extent (see table 5).

Table 5: Intention (panel)

Male				Panel	Female			
AM 2006	AM 2007	Δ AM 06-07	Corr. Δ AM		AM 2006	AM 2007	Δ AM 06-07	Corr. Δ AM
1.80	2.00	-0.2	0.856	**Intention**	1.71	2.00	-.29 °	0.582

° significance at 0.05 level

In discordance to the panel findings, women and men differ significantly in the founding intention in each survey within the study cohort. Men have thought about becoming self-employed to a higher extent than women (see table 6).

Table 6: Intention (study cohort)

Male				Study cohort	Female			
AM 2006	n	AM 2007	n		AM 2006	n	AM 2007	n
2.28 °	108	2.22 °	73	**Intention**	1.80 °	117	1.79 °	108

° significance at 0.05 level

3.4.2 Motives for Becoming Self-employed

In general, male and female participants of the panel group evaluate motives towards self-employment in a similar way (see table 3.1). Although means tend to differ notably (e.g. better opportunity self-realisation), within the panel group no significant differences could be identified in the conducted surveys between the two gender. However, male and female participants have changed in their evaluation of motives from winter term 2006 to winter 2007. Men rated in the second study, "to put studies into action" more neutral in the context of becoming self-employed. Women perceived the economic climate less fostering. Regarding the motive "continue family business" women changed their assessment towards tending to disagree with this motive after one year (see table 7).

Table 7: Motives (panel)

Male				Panel	Female			
AM 2006	AM 2007	Δ AM 06-07	Corr. Δ AM	Motives [1]	AM 2006	AM 2007	Δ AM 06-07	Corr. Δ AM
2.79	3.26	-0.47	0.537 *	Continue family busi- ness	2.74	3.33	-0.58°	0.549*
2.53	3.00	-0.47 °	0.616 *	Put studied into action	2.73	2.54	0.19	0.465*
2.83	3.00	-0.17	0.323	Good eco- nomic climate	2.49	2.84	-0.35°	0.49*

scale used: (from 1= totally agree to 5= totally disagree), ° significance at 0.05 level; * significance at 0.05 level for correlations

In contrast to the panel findings, three significant differences could be identified in the cohort group between the gender in the first survey. "Better opportunity for self-realisation", "continue family business" and "good economic" climate were all significant on a 5% level. In addition, women showed a higher tendency to agree that these factors are motives towards self-employment. After one year, however, these items showed no significance in the second survey. Instead "po-tential profit" was significant and was rated higher by men (see table 8).

Table 8: Motives (study cohort)

Male				Study cohort	Female			
AM 2006	n	AM 2007	n	Motives [1]	AM 2006	n	AM 2007	n
2.11°	110	1.96	81	Better opportunity for self-realisation	1.75°	123	2.01	111
1.92	109	2.11°	81	Potential profit	2.10	122	2.38°	111
3.35°	109	3.53	80	Continue family business	2.82°	114	3.16	105
2.81°	107	3.05	79	Good economic climate	2.55°	121	2.93	107

scale used: (from 1= totally agree to 5= totally disagree), ° significance (2-tailed) at 0.05 level; * significance at 0.05 level for correlations

Interestingly, exactly those items were found significant in the cohort analysis, which had already recognisable but not significant differences in the mean within the panel group. An explanation could be that the number of panel participants was too small in size. As the panel results have shown that "continue family business" and "good economic climate" have changed significantly and became, therefore, less important for women, it could explain why both factors were not found significant between the two gender in the cohort analysis.

3.4.3 Motives against Becoming Self-employed (Perceived Hurdles)

Male and female participants perceive most of the hindering factors similar. At the beginning differences exist in the panel with "bad economic climate", "bound to the own company" and "missing social appreciation". Male panel members tend to see those factors less problematic as their female counterparts. Regarding "bound to the own company" a convergence can be identified so that no significant difference exists within the second survey. Over time only one significant change can be found in the valuation of the variable "missing seed capital" of men as scepticism increases. For female respondents three significant developments can be found. "Missing founding partner/team", "low income" and "risk of failure" are seen more optimistic after one year (see table 9).

Table 9: Hindering factors (panel)

Male				Panel	Female			
AM 2006	AM 2007	Δ AM 06-07	Corr. Δ AM	Hindering Factors [1]	AM 2006	AM 2007	Δ AM 06-07	Corr. Δ AM
2.40	1.80	0.60 °	0.521 *	Missing seed capital	2.36	2.14	0.22	0.679*
3.21	3.37	-0.16	0.137	Missing founding partner /team	2.92	3.39	-0.47 °	0.622*
3.32	3.11	0.21	-0.062	Low income	2.83	3.23	-0.40 °	0.494*
3.06°	3.56°	-0.50	0.521	Bad economic climate	2.42°	2.67°	-0.24	0.407*
3.95°	3.63	0.32	0.156	Bound to the own company	3.16°	3.35	-0.19	0.179
2.60	2.35	0.25	0.309	Risk of failure	2.24	2.67	-0.46°	0.308
4.37°	4.37°	0.00	0.236	Missing social appreciation	3.66°	3.83°	-0.17	0.163

[1] scale used: (from 1= totally agree to 5= totally disagree), o significance (2-tailed) at 0.05 leve; * significance at 0.05 level for correlations

In general women perceive the hindering factors in the cohort study as more problematic than men. Furthermore, the differences between male and female participants are larger than in the panel. In the first survey "missing market knowledge", "high financial risk", "bad economic climate" "bound to the own company" and "risk of failure" were significantly different between the gender. In the second survey significance could be found for "missing business knowledge", "high financial risk", "general missing interest", "too much work and too less spare-time", "bad economic climate", "bound to the own company" and "risk of failure" (see table 10).

Table 10: Hindering factors (Study cohort)

Male				Study cohort	Female			
AM 2006	n	AM 2007	n	Hindering Factors [1]	AM 2006	n	AM 2007	n
3.04	107	3.44 °	82	Missing business knowledge	2.72	118	3.06 °	109
3.29	107	3.50°	80	Missing interest	2.93	109	2.89°	111
2.67°	108	2.67	81	Missing market knowledge	2.33°	118	2.45	109
2.40°	108	2.29°	79	High financial risk	2.04°	119	1.89°	109
2.79	107	3.05°	78	Too much work and too less spare-time	2.54	118	2.64°	109
2.99°	104	3.29°	75	Bad economic climate	2.55°	117	2.76°	102
3.42°	106	3.45.°	78	Bound to the own company	3.08°	118	3.10°	109
2.56°	106	2.61 °	80	Risk of failure	2.23°	119	1.95°	110

scale used: (from 1= totally agree to 5= totally disagree), ° significance (2-tailed) at 0.05 level; *
significance at 0.05 level for correlations

For the item "bad economic climate", the independent t-tests in the panel and
cohort analysis showed differences between the gender, as women see the economic climate less positive than men. However, the respondents tend to disagree
with the statement that economic climate is seen as hindering. An explanation
could be that the economy in Germany was and is in a growth phase. "Bound to
the own company" was also significant in both approaches. Although, changes
over time could be found in the panel they can not give an indication for the different values in the cohort study.

3.5   Regression Analyses

For the panel study the results of the regression analyses are presented in the following. Regression analysis was conducted using as independent variables the
three motives which became significant in the t-tests as well as the four hurdles
which showed significant differences between survey 1 and 2 (see table 3). As
controls gender was inserted into the model. For survey 1 and survey 2 no differences were found between the gender, i.e. the control variable did not become
significant. Regarding the independent variables, the results demonstrated "risk
of failure" as the dominant hurdle throughout the years. No other independent
variable showed a significant effect (5% level). For survey 1 "good economic
climate" had an additional effect on intention (10% level) and for survey 2 "missing founding partner/team" influences founding intention (10% level). The entire
model reached an R^2 of 24.4% (significant on the 10% level) for survey 1 and
36.5% (significant on the 5% level) for survey 2 (see table 11).

Table 11: Panel findings for regression analyses with motives and hurdles

	SURVEY 1		SURVEY 2	
	Model 1 (Controls)	Model 2 (+ IVs)	Model 1 (Controls)	Model 2 (+ IVs)
Main effects				
risk of failure		-.351**		-.412**
low income		-.200		-.129
missing partner/team		.067		-.211*
missing seed capital		-.110		-.178
succession		-.019		.160
put studied into action		.015		-.001
good economic climate		-.277*		-.116
Control variables				
Gender (0,1)	-.108	-.019	-.056	-.014
Model				
R Square:	1.20%	24.40%	0.30%	36.50%

* p<0.10; ** p<0.05; N= 58

For the second regression analysis the family background was inserted. In general the proportion of self-employed fathers was higher than of self-employed mothers in the panel (see table 2). The percentage of female participants with a self-employed father is higher than of their male counterparts, while slightly more men than women have self-employed mothers. For survey 1 the entire model with gender, self-employed father and mother reached an R2 of 13.7% but did not become significant on the 5% level but on the 10% level (see table 6). No significant gender differences could be found. However the results showed mother's self-employment as the only significant variable (beta = .349) within this regression (5% level). For survey 2 the entire model attained an R^2 of 13.9%

and became significant on the 10% level (similar to study 1). Regarding the affecting variables this time, father's self-employment became significant (beta=.328) on the 5% level. Again no significant gender differences could be found (see table 12).

Table 12: Panel findings for regression analyses with family background

	SURVEY 1		SURVEY 2	
	Model 1 (Controls)	Model 2 (+ IVs)	Model 1 (Controls)	Model 2 (+ IVs)
Main effects				
father's self-employment		.115		.328**
mother's self-employment		.349**		.233
Control variables				
Gender (0,1)	-.187	-.065	-.133	-.053
Model				
R Square:	3.5%	13.7%	1.8%	13.9%

* p<0.10; ** p<0.05; N= 58

3.6   Discussion and Limitations

Regarding intention, men seem to have a higher interest in becoming self-employed, even if significance for this was only found in the cohort analysis. This finding is in accordance with previous research conducted on potential entrepreneurs (students) (see Chen et al., 1998). Only small differences could be found between the two gender in motives for becoming self-employed. Significant changes over time in the panel group could partly give an indication why existing significant differences in the cross-sectional analysis in the cohort occurred. The identified motives "better opportunity for self-realisation", "continue family business" and "good economic" (study 1) and "potential profit" (study 2) besides are not completely in concordance with the existing literature. Status e.g.

was perceived similar by male and female participants. In general, it can be stated that women perceive hindering factors more problematic than their male counterparts. However, only within the perception of hindering factors especially the cohort analysis showed that the two gender differ in many aspects. The regression analyses showed that the risk of failure is a dominant and stable hurdle throughout the years which prevents most of the sample from becoming self-employed. Here, no differences could be found between men and women. It could be also shown that the self-employment of the parents does have an influence on the founding intention of the offspring. Next to family background, some research is indicating a positive relationship between entrepreneurship education and the intention to start a business (Peterman & Kennedy, 2003; Lee & Wong, 2003; Kolvereid & Moen, 1997).Within this study entrepreneurial education could not be analysed as the numbers of students who have attended entrepreneurship lectures or seminars are quite small (below 10) and do not allow further analyses (t-tests or regression analyses). Future research could analyse the effect of entrepreneurship education on the intention to start a business, after participants had specific entrepreneurship lectures.

The selection of a single country has the obvious limitation that the results generalise across populations and geographical settings. Furthermore, the survey was only conducted at the University of Erlangen-Nuremberg, which could affect the explanatory content. Another bias could be based on the fact that participants have chosen mainly business administration as their major. Therefore, it would be necessary to include also students from different faculties into the survey sample to exclude study-related biases. With 28 male and 30 female respondents the panel size was small in size (therefore the results of the regression analyses should only be looked upon as tendencies). Although cross-sectional findings were compared with the general study cohort resulting biases could have influenced the results. The second survey was conducted in the third study semester which marks the middle of the bachelor study programme. Further surveys could enable a further look whether students' intention to become self-employed has been realised or not. Hence, future research shall consider gender related differences in the founding intentions as an essential factor for improving entrepreneurship education.

4   Gender-related Differences in Goals and Performance Evaluation?

4.1   Introduction

Following Krueger et al. (2000), intentions are the best predictors of planned behaviour in psychology. Several intention models already exist in literature, however, the most cited one is Ajzen's (1991) theory of planned behaviour. This theory identifies three antecedents of intention: attitude towards the behaviour, subjective norms and perceived feasibility (Krueger et al., 2000). Having the theory of planned behaviour as a background, an effort is made in this chapter to explore motives towards self-employment, working goals and success evaluation. Those aspects reflect or at least influence subjective norms and the perceived feasibility and can be, hence, seen as antecedents of the students' career choice and in extension their intention to become entrepreneurs.

Attention is also given to gender similarities or differences in the working goals of students. Since the 1980's, a considerable amount of research has been conducted in the field of female entrepreneurship. However, research on female entrepreneurs suffers from a number of shortcomings such as a lack of theoretical grounding, the neglect of structural, historical, and cultural factors (Ahl, 2006). The above mentioned shortcomings could also be a reason why current literature on gender differences in entrepreneurship is full of mixed and contradictory results. There seems to be no consensus among scholars whether small, large or if differences at all exist between male and female entrepreneurs. It is however a fact that over the last twenty years, academics and economic organisations have demonstrated a growing interest in women entrepreneurs, especially in the United States and Canada due to their economic importance (Becker-Blease & Sohl, 2007).

Furthermore, most studies on gender and entrepreneurship focus on existing entrepreneurs. Alsos and Ljunggren (1998) argue that "at this stage the gender imbalance is already materialised, and the (male and female) respondents in the studies are only those who succeeded in setting up a business" (p. 138).Bearing this in mind, another approach has been chosen to try to identify differences or similarities among the two gender at a specific phase (during their studies), where they have the potential to become entrepreneurs and situational factors (e.g., unemployment or worse career opportunities) that could occur after the commencement of business activities have not been experienced yet, and can not influence the selection of the professional career (self-employment or not).

To sum up, the aim of this chapter is to look at gender related differences regarding the goals that are associated and pursued in the context of business foundation. Special attention will be paid to three different aspects. First, the goals that illustrate the system of objectives pursued in the working life by women and men will be analysed. Secondly, an analysis will be conducted of how women and men perceive the success of a newly founded company in general and the success of their own (potential) company in particular. Potential changes of the above mentioned aspects will also be researched over time to get a closer look at the process of venture creation thus satisfying the need for panel studies in the entrepreneurship research.

4.2   Theoretical Perspective and Research Questions

4.2.1   Students as a Focus in the Entrepreneurial Research

Various scholars identified the need to find the antecedents of students' career choice and researched several antecedents as for example personal and situational factors. Singh and DeNoble (2003) found that personality (BIG 5), gender and having a close self-employed relative, altogether have a strong positive relation to attitude on self-employment. Scott and Twomey (1988), Kolvereid (1996), Lüthje and Franke (2003), Kourilsky and Walstad (1998), Wang and Wong (2004) have empirically researched students' attitudes towards entrepreneurship. Their findings indicate that interest and actual behaviour can not be seen synonymously. Therefore, it is important to research the factors that may affect the career choice of students. In contrast, Lee and Wong (2003) found that there is a positive relationship between entrepreneurship education and the intention to start a business. This was also found and confirmed by the study of Souitaris et al. (2007). Motives and working goals have attracted less attention while there are studies that have been concentrated on perceived inhibiting factors towards the career choice of students (e.g. Görisch et al., 2002). In 1984, Klandt showed that the micro-social environment and namely the family background affect the founding intention and activity. Furthermore, he found that the father's profession has an effect on the occupational decision of the son and the daughter, while the mother's influence is limited to the daughter. There are other studies that have also taken gender into consideration as a possible factor affecting entrepreneurial intention. It has been found that male students have a higher intention to become entrepreneurs than their female counterparts (e.g. Wang & Wong, 2004; Matthews & Moser, 1996). Furthermore, female students' entrepreneurial goals were centred on helping the community, while males' goals focused on growing beyond a single unit and to support their families (Terjesen & Shay, 2005). However, these empirical results must be seen before the background of the individual study design, especially what kind of population was selected.

The study presented in this chapter has the goal to continue the work conducted until now, especially on youth entrepreneurship, and to complement it by presenting potential changes through time (panel study). So as to understand the entrepreneurial process it is important to research potential entrepreneurs (Matthews & Moser, 1996). However, in order to have a broader view, it is considered also important to give an overview of existing (male and female) entrepreneurs, their characteristics, motives and working goals.

4.2.2   Male and Female Entrepreneurs in General

In 1986, Stevenson posed the question: whether theory that is developed from research on male-led ventures hold true for women and minority entrepreneurs. Scholars like Fischer et al. (1993) have suggested the use of feminism approaches. They suggest that the perspectives of liberal and social feminism can help in understanding the nature and implication of issues related to gender and entrepreneurship. The social feminism perspective (rooted from social learning theory to psychoanalysis) argues that men and women are fundamentally the same, but males and females differ in their points of view due to different experiences from the earliest moments of life. The theory of liberal feminism (rooted in the liberal political theory) suggests that women are underprivileged compared with men because of discrimination or other factors that e.g. prevent them from studying or from gaining working experience (Fischer, 1993). As social feminism is seen as the more appropriate theory to explain gender-related differences (Fischer et al., 1993) it will serve as basis for this chapter.

Brush's (1992) literature review shows that there are more gender similarities than gender differences in individual characteristics such as demographic characteristics and business skills. However, gender related differences have been found in several entrepreneurship aspects such as business and industry choices, financing strategies, growth patterns, and governance structures (Greene et al., 2003; Hisrich & O'Brien, 1982). Females develop different products, pursue different goals, need less credit and launch their businesses on a smaller scale (Fischer et al., 1993; Chaganti & Parasuraman, 1996; Carter et al., 1997; Verheul, 2003). Besides that women judge their knowledge, experience and success lower than men (Sternberg et al., 2004). In comparison to men, women are more risk averse and spend less time on networking (Rosa et al., 1996; Verheul & Thurik, 2001).

4.2.3 Working Goals

The term motive has been defined in psychology as a recurrent concern for a goal state that is based on a natural incentive – a concern that energises, orients and selects behaviour (McClelland, 1987).

Using several methods such as interviews or psychometric scales researchers have tried to identify what motivates to become an entrepreneur (Cromie, 1987). Using interviews they came up to motives like: autonomy, achievement, making money, desire to exploit a market opportunity, frustration with last job, frustration with career etc. Using psychometric scales they found that achievement and autonomy are important motives. Especially looking at McClelland's empirical studies one can see that the need of achievement is a key motive that drives entrepreneurs.

Till the mid eighties studies on the motives of female entrepreneurs were scarce. According to Birley (1989) it is "clear that from the literature the motivation of female entrepreneurs is similar in most respects to those of their male counterparts" As to whether male and female entrepreneurs have different motives as far as entrepreneurship is concerned, results seem to be rather contradicting as there are researchers that argue there are no differences between the two gender and others that indeed found differences (e.g. Schwartz, 1976; Cromie, 1987).

Schwartz (1976) found that women entrepreneurs were motivated by achievement, autonomy, enhanced job satisfaction and the desire to make money. Goffee and Scase (1985) detected that women establish a business in order to escape from domestic and labour market subordination but they found no differences between men and women in three motives: avoiding low paid occupation, escaping supervision and the constraint of subservient roles. Using interviews Cromie in his study of 1987 found independence to be a strong motivator for both males and females and that achievement and status were equally important for males and females. Regarding independence as a motivator to become self-employed, no gender differences have also been found by Shane et al. (1991). Money was a significant and stronger motivator for men while career dissatisfaction and child rearing was a stronger motivator for women (Shane et al., 1991). Financial gain was also in the study of Bradley and Boles (2003) a strong motivation for males in general and less for women (Bradley & Boles, 2003). Scott (1986) reported that also women were also concerned about personal challenge and satisfaction, while men stressed the need to be their own bosses. Women are less likely than male entrepreneurs to be motivated by advancement, but rather by family and lifestyle (DeMartino & Barbato, 2003). Other studies emphasise the importance of self-accomplishment and quality of life (Bennett & Dann, 2000; Bradley & Boles, 2003). The three most important factors influencing women in becoming entrepreneurs are according to Ufuk and Oezgen (2001): meeting the family needs, initiating social relations, and self-fulfilment. However, these partially contradicting results can be due to different research designs as well.

According to Baum and Locke (2004) in the literature it has been suggested that there are at least three motivation factors that have an effect on the performance of a business. These are: goals, vision and self-efficacy. In this chapter working goals are being researched as a more concrete form of motivation (this is a reason that in some cases motives and goals are interrelated) that could drive students towards entrepreneurship, as goals are also said to be good predictors of planned behaviour (Bagozzi et al., 1989). Goals have been defined by Bandura (1986) as the determination to engage in a particular activity and are seen by Segal et al. (2007) as an important aspect of many career choice and decision-making theories. Goals have also been recognised to play an important role in venture growth (Covin & Slevin, 1997) and new venture survival (Carsrud & Krueger, 1995).

Studies on the motives and working goals of potential entrepreneurs (students) with a gender focus have been scarce in entrepreneurship literature. Under the basic assumption of social feminism that women differ fundamentally from men due to their socialisation, it is necessary to analyse how gender affects motivation and working goals. Furthermore, Mueller (2004) suggests that whereas retrospective (post-venture creation) studies find no or little differences between men and women entrepreneurs, it could be that prospective studies (pre-venture creation) could show that there are indeed significant differences in the motivation, goals, intention, etc. between the two gender.

Therefore the following research questions are posed:

Research question 1: Do male and female students differ in their working goals?

Research question 2: Do male and female students have over time stable working goals?

4.2.4 Success Perception

The exact definition of the term success is complex in the context of entrepreneurship and especially if the effort is made to compare two gender. So it is partly contradictory to classify if and particularly when a business foundation can be considered as successful. Hence, "success is an evaluative concept", and research in this area has to include to whom and by what criteria a given indicator implies success (Jaskolka & Beyer, 1985).

However, there is a certain consensus that the business foundation success is determined by several different factors. In general, these criteria can be summarised in four main categories: efficiency/profitability, size, growth and personality, of which efficiency and growth are used most in literature (Voigt & Brem, 2007). Moreover, research indicates that success and the individual perception of success changes over time (Weber & Schaper, 2004). A common approach in this area is to predict success and failure probability of companies (e.g. Lussier & Pfeifer, 2001).

The perception of success is strongly dependant on the personal subjective estimation. This awareness becomes even more different if people from different regions and age-groups are researched. The target group comprises students that most probably have not founded until now a company. Instead of including the well researched notion of company success, the notion of success perception was included. In this context, students mostly focus on their subjective and objective career success. This focus is taken as well in for to-date research in this area on the conceptualisation and evaluation of career success (Heslin, 2005).

Directly asked for their success perception ("What does it mean for you to be successful in your business"), women entrepreneurs define the company's success mainly in increased revenues and profits, as a function of their environment, and in relation to their own situation (Lee-Gosselin & Grisé, 1990)

Within this chapter the success of an own (potential) and somebody else's business was asked from the participants to examine whether the success of an own or somebody else's business is understood differently. While the success of a company that was founded by someone else could be evaluated on concepts learned during the study and corresponds with a perceived common understanding of success and hence, mirror prevailing norms, the success of an own (potential) business start-up could reveal and reflect the individual understanding of success of a respondent.

Therefore the following research questions are posed:

Research question 3: Do male and female students differ in their success understanding of somebody else's business start-up?

Research question 4: Do male and female students have over time a stable success understanding of somebody else's business start-up?

Research question 5: Do male and female students differ in their success understanding of their own (potential) business start-up?

Research question 6: Do male and female students have over time a stable success understanding of their own (potential) business start-up?

4.2.5 Longitudinal Studies

Less effort has been made in entrepreneurship literature to catch a glimpse of entrepreneurial related variables as they occur over time. Matthews and Moser (1996), however, argue that these "processes are best studied prospectively and over time." Hence, their point of view that by asking potential and not existing entrepreneurs a researcher can better understand the process of deciding to start a business is also followed in this study. They found that male students were more interested in founding their business and that the difference in this interest grew over time. However, to the authors' knowledge, longitudinal studies that have students as a focus are rare (e.g. Matthews & Moser, 1996). In literature which deals with existing entrepreneurs, some studies that use longitudinal data can be found. In 1983, Hisrich and Brush undertook the first longitudinal study on female entrepreneurship conducted in the US (Greene et al, 2003).

4.3   Methodology

4.3.1 Data Collection and Sample Characteristics

Two surveys were conducted between winter term 2006/2007 and winter term 2007/2008 at the University of Erlangen-Nuremberg. In total 553 students participated in the first and 398 in the second survey. The questionnaires were handed out in lectures that are mainly visited in successive order during the study. For the purpose of this chapter only data from bachelor students will be used who have started their study in the winter term 2006/2007. On average the participating student was born 1985 and was studying Business Administration (see figure 20).

Following Hakim (2000) the sample fulfils the requirements of a cohort study. The first wave (study I) included 243 students at the start of their study. The proportion of male and female respondents was almost even with 120 men and 122 women. 195 could be allocated in following survey (study II) to this group. Therefore the cohort study includes 243, respectively 195 participants for the two waves. From the entire sample 20 male and 38 female respondents could be identified for a panel study (n=58).

Figure 20: Data collection and sample characteristics

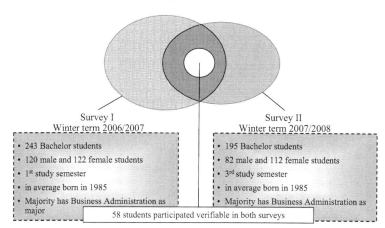

Survey I	Survey II
Winter term 2006/2007	Winter term 2007/2008
• 243 Bachelor students	• 195 Bachelor students
• 120 male and 122 female students	• 82 male and 112 female students
• 1st study semester	• 3rd study semester
• in average born in 1985	• in average born in 1985
• Majority has Business Administration as major	• Majority has Business Administration as

58 students participated verifiable in both surveys

4.3.2 Operationalisation of the Variables

Working Goals

For the measurement of working goals the question: "How important are the following goals for your working life?" was used (Schenk, 1998, in Frese, 1998).
The scale contains 16 different goals. The areas of goals vary from finance goals
to social and independence goals. An example item is: "self-actualisation". Answers ranged between 1 (=very important) and 5 (=not important at all) (see table
14).

Table 14: Working life goals

Self-realisation/ realise own ideas	Work contributing to innovations	Profit
Independency	Achieve influence	Work climate/ satisfied employees
Good/ high income	Contact to interesting people	Company's growth
Good carrier opportunities	Create something sustainable	Revenue
Widen own horizon	Status/prestige	Helping people with work
Work-life-balance	Being better than competitors	Boost people
Challenging task	Satisfied customers	Secure job(s)

Success evaluation

Items for the evaluation of a business start-up or rather a newly founded business were drawn from literature (e.g. Cliff, 1998; Chell & Baines, 1998; Ziegerer, 1993; Loscocco et al., 1991; Boden & Nucci, 2000; Klandt, 1984 etc.). 14 success criteria were included in the questionnaire, which comprise economical and non-economical aspects. The question used was "How do you assess following criteria to evaluate the success of a business start-up or newly founded company?" and respondents could choose between the answer alternatives from 1 (= very important) to 6 (=completely unimportant). This question was asked in respect to somebody else's business and afterwards (hypothetical) to their own (see table 15).

Table 15: Success evaluation criteria

Revenue	Employee satisfaction	Employee motivation
Number of employees	Work climate	Durability
Profit	Offered social benefits	Company's image
Market share	Company's growth	Status symbols
Entrepreneurial profit	Secure jobs	

4.4   Results

In the following chapter at first the statistical results for the panel will be illustrated, afterwards the results from the study cohort will be presented and the results of both approaches will be compared. Independent t-tests were conducted to find differences between men and women for each survey in panel and study cohort. Paired t-tests were chosen to identify and analyse changes and development over time and were done separately for men and women for the panel. Figure 21 and 22 summarise the research framework for the panel and the cohort study.

Figure 21: Research framework (panel)

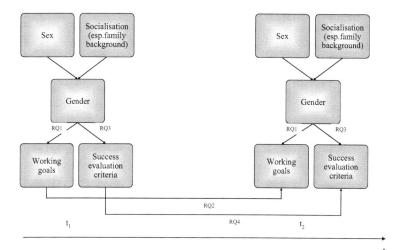

Figure 22: Research framework (cohort study)

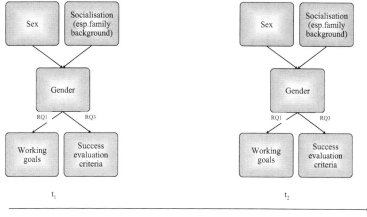

4.4.1 Working Goals

Male and female panel samples evaluate goals mainly similar. They distinguish at the beginning of this study only to the extent to which three factors are perceived. While the male group emphasised the meaning of profit, the female group saw satisfied customers and a secure job as more important. After one year the attitude of the men towards profit has changed as it became less important for them. As a result profit was equally important for men and women in the second survey. Women also changed their assessment over time as "work contributing to innovations", "prestige" and "being better than competitors" lost importance. These changes had however no significant influence on the evaluation of those factors between the gender. Men and women rated "profit", "being better than competitors" as important, while "work contributing to innovations" was rather seen as neutral (see table 18).

Table 18: Working goals (panel)

Male				Panel	Female			
AM 2006	AM 2007	Δ AM 06-07	Corr. Δ AM	Working goals	AM 2006	AM 2007	Δ AM 06-07	Corr. Δ AM
2.89	3.20	-0.26	0.219	Work contributing to innova-	2.76	3.18	-0.42°	0.644 *
2.15	2.45	-0.30	0.700 *	Status/ prestige	2.55	2.92	-0.41°	0.487 *
2.30	2.75	-0.45	0.643 *	Being better than competitors	2.42	2.87	-0.45°	0.440 *
2.20°	2.30°	-0.10	0.243	Satisfied customers	1.66°	1.82°	-0.16	0.410 *

scale used: (from 1= very important to 6= totally unimportant); ° significance (2-tailed) at 0.05 level for the paired and independent t-test; * significance at 0.05 level for correlations

Within the analysis of the study cohort also goals are found significant that posses a notable mean difference already in the panel analysis, but not on a significant level. "Widen own horizon", "work-life-balance", "status/prestige", "work climate/satisfied customers" and "helping people with work" as well as "secure job(s)" were all found significant. Over time only four ("work-life-balance", "work climate/satisfied customers", "helping people with work", "secure jobs") were stable and were identified as well in the findings of the second survey after one year. Additionally, also "satisfied customers" was significant (see table 3). Apart from "status/prestige" all criteria were rated by female respondents as more important than by their male counterparts in the 2007/2008 survey (see table 19).

Table 19: Working goals (study cohort)

Male				Study cohort	Female			
AM 2006	n	AM 2007	n	Working goals	AM 2006	n	AM 2007	n
2.26°	117	2.22	82	Widen own horizon	1.83°	123	2.05	110
2.35°	118	2.47°	81	Work-life-balance	1.80°	124	1.74°	112
2.25°	116	2.60	81	Status/ prestige	2.56°	124	2.62	111
2.18	114	2.24°	76	Satisfied customers	1.94	124	1.92°	112
1.81°	114	1.85°	78	Work climate/ satisfied employees	1.50°	121	1.49°	110
2.77°	115	2.96°	78	Helping people with work	2.30°	122	2.29°	112
2.25°	114	2.53°	80	Secure job(s)	1.60°	121	1.67°	111

scale used: (from 1= very important to 6= totally unimportant); ° significance (2-tailed) at 0.05 level for the paired and independent t-test; * significance at 0.05 level for correlations

4.4.2 Success Evaluation

Success Evaluation (Somebody Else's Business)

Regarding the success evaluation of somebody else's business no differences existed at the beginning in the panel group. In the follow-up survey the male and female respondents distinguished themselves in the assessment of "revenue" and "market share". Women rated the "market share" and "revenue" as success criteria higher than their male counterparts. The significant difference in "market share" could be based on the changed attitude of men that occurred over time. Women also changed their evaluation over time towards "offered social benefits" and "employee motivation". Despite those changes, men and women evaluated those items equally as a more neutral success criterion (see table 20).

Table 20: Success evaluation (somebody else's) (panel)

Male				Panel	Female			
AM 2006	AM 2007	Δ AM 06-07	Corr. Δ AM	Success evaluation (s. e.)	AM 2006	AM 2007	Δ AM 06-07	Corr. Δ AM
2.50	2.85°	-0.35	0.366	Revenue	2.18	2.18°	0.00°	0.319
2.75	3.50°	-0.75°	0.478*	Market share	2.71	2.79°	-0.08	0.358*
2.89	3.10	-0.32	0.566*	Offered social benefits	2.39	2.79	-0.39°	0.431*
1.63	1.65	-0.03	0.159	Employee motivation	1.71	1.45	0.26°	0.463*

scale used: (from 1= very important to 6= totally unimportant) ° significance at 0.05 (2-tailed) level for the paired and independent t-test; * significance at 0.05 level for correlations

In the study cohort, "offered social benefits" and "secure jobs" were at the beginning significantly rated higher by women than men. In the second survey, "secure jobs" showed no significance. Instead women differed significantly from men in the criteria "number of employees", "market share", "entrepreneurial profit", "offered social benefits", "employee satisfaction", "work climate", "company's growth", "employee motivation", "durability", "company's image" and "status symbols". Interestingly, women evaluated all ten criteria more important for the evaluation of success of somebody else's business than men (see table 21).

Table 21: Success evaluation (somebody else's) (study cohort)

Male				Study cohort	Female			
AM 2006	n	AM 2007	n	Success evaluation (s. e.)	AM 2006	n	AM 2007	n
3.41	115	3.65°	81	Number of employees	3.27	122	3.35°	112
2.86	114	3.20°	81	Market share	2.59	120	2.79°	112
2.10	114	2.15°	81	Employee satisfaction	1.86	121	1.83°	110
1.95	114	2.15°	81	Work climate	1.74	121	1.72°	109
2.95°	111	3.41°	81	Offered social benefits	2.44°	122	2.50°	111
1.96	113	1.94°	81	Company's growth	1.93	122	1.92°	112
2.34°	113	2.78	81	Secure jobs	1.93°	121	2.11	112
1.66	112	1.81°	80	Employee motivation	1.73	121	1.65°	110
2.00	113	1.95°	81	Durability	1.76	122	1.69°	110
2.03	112	2.35°	81	Company's image	1.96	123	2.04°	112
3.42	114	3.99°	81	Status symbols	3.28	122	3.61°	112

scale used: (from 1= very important to 6= totally unimportant); ° significance (2-tailed) at 0.05 level for the paired and independent t-test; * significance at 0.05 level for correlations

The comparison of panel and cohort results can give hints why "offered social benefits" were not found significant in the cohort results anymore as women have changed over time in this aspect according to the panel analysis. In a similar way, it could be explained why "market share" was different between the gender in the second survey as men have changed significantly over time in this item.

Success Evaluation (Own Company)

Results regarding the evaluation of an own (potential) business and somebody else's do not differ fundamentally. Similar to the results for the success evaluation of somebody else's business no significant differences could be identified at the beginning between male and female panel members in the success evaluation of their own (potential) business. The findings regarding the importance of "revenue" and "market share" in the second survey, can be found as well in the success evaluation of an own business, as women tend to perceive "revenue" and "market share" as more important. "Offered social benefits" illustrates a significant difference between male and female participants in the second survey. The reason for this change is explained by men's change over time in this aspect. Male participants reduced their valuation of this aspect over time on a significant base (see table 22).

Table 22: Success evaluation (own) (panel)

Male				Panel	Female			
AM 2006	AM 2007	ΔAM 06-07	Corr. Δ AM	Success evaluation (own business)	AM 2006	AM 2007	ΔAM 06-07	Corr. Δ AM
2.25	2.80°	-0.55	0.108	Revenue	2.12	2.08°	0.15	0.471*
2.70	3.25°	-0.55°	0.588 *	Market share	2.47	2.47°	0.06	0.272
2.85	3.40°	-0.55°	0.600 *	Offered social benefits	2.44	2.71°	-0.15	0.375*

scale used: (from 1= very important to 6= totally unimportant); ° significance (2-tailed) at 0.05 level for the paired and independent t-test; * significance at 0.05 level for correlations

Within the study cohort "offered social benefits", "employee motivation" and "durability" were significantly different between in the gender at the beginning. Within the second survey after one year "revenue", "number of employees", "market share", "employee satisfaction", "work climate", "offered social benefits" as well as "secure jobs" were significantly differently evaluated by men and women (see table 23).

Table 23: Success evaluation (own) (study cohort)

Male				Study cohort	Female			
AM 2006	n	AM 2007	n	Success evaluation (own business)	AM 2006	n	AM 2007	n
2.21	109	2.42°	81	Revenue	2.06	118	2.12°	110
3.22	110	3.59°	81	Number of employees	3.10	116	3.23°	110
2.71	109	2.95°	81	Market share	2.41	116	2.49°	110
2.01	110	2.15°	81	Employee satisfaction	1.79	116	1.73°	106
1.80	108	1.99°	81	Work climate	1.74	117	1.62°	107
3.04°	109	3.51°	81	Offered social benefits	2.51°	116	2.50°	110
2.33°	110	2.77°	81	Secure jobs	2.02°	115	1.99°	109
2.11°	108	1.91°	81	Durability	1.75°	118	1.64°	108

scale used: (from 1= very important to 6= totally unimportant); ° significance (2-tailed) at 0.05 level for the paired and independent t-test; * significance at 0.05 level for correlations

The comparison of cohort with panel results shows that those criteria are found significant in the cohort that were already notably different but not significantly different in the panel. "Revenue", "market share" and "offered social benefits" were found in both groups significant between the gender. Identified changes in the panel over time could explain why "offered social benefits", "market share", "employee satisfaction" and "durability" were not stable between the surveys in the cohort analysis. For female panel members the importance of "employee satisfaction" and "durability" decreased. Male panel members rated "offered social benefits" and "market share" more important.

4.5   Discussion and Conclusion

In this chapter, it was tried to gain a deeper understanding of the effect of gender on the business goals, as well as on the success evaluation of a potential company. Drawing from data on 243 (survey 1) and 195 (survey 2) students (cohort study), respectively 58 students (panel study),it was found that male and female participants differ in less areas than expected. Even more importantly, it was found that both groups showed similar tendencies over time. The findings on potential entrepreneurs are in accordance with literature on existing entrepreneurs that argues that there are more similarities than differences among the two gender (Birley, 1989; Brush, 1992; Green et al., 2003).

Mueller (2004) suggested that whereas post-venture creation studies find no or little differences between men and women entrepreneurs, it could be that prospective studies pre-venture creation could show that there are indeed significant differences between the two gender. Results in the comparison of working goals of panel and cohort are not mutual exclusive. However, interesting hints for the development are offered by the panel analysis. Men seem to evaluate the meaning of profit lower after one year and approximate to the evaluation of women. Within the cohort analysis women tend to value social and personal development goals at the beginning higher than their male counterparts. After one year, though, differences partly disappear, and only "satisfied customers", "satisfied employees" and "work-life-balance" differ significantly.

Results in the evaluation of somebody else's business start-up and (potential) one's own are similar, even if more significant differences could be identified in the cohort analysis. Interestingly, few differences exist in general in the first study and numerous in the second. Especially women rate success criteria as more important than men (e.g. revenue, market share, offered social benefits).

The presented study has, however, some limitations. The selection of a single country has the limitation regarding the generalisation of the results across populations and geographical settings. Furthermore, the survey was only conducted at the University of Erlangen-Nuremberg, which could affect the explanatory content. Another bias could be based on the fact that participants have chosen mainly business administration as their major. Therefore, it would be necessary to include also students from different faculties into the survey sample to exclude study-related biases. Especially the evaluation of the success of a company could be influenced by lectures visited during the study. With 28 male and 30 female respondents the panel size was small in size. Although the cross-sectional findings of the panel were compared with the general study cohort, the small size could have influenced the results. Future surveys could analyse whether professional working goals change more towards the end of the study programme as the evaluation has a direct impact on the job decision.

To sum up, the question remains when the differences between males and females occur. The social feminism perspective argues that men and women are fundamentally the same, but males and females differ in their points of view due to different experiences from the earliest moments of life. However in the study that has been conducted in a rather early point of the life of the respondents only minor differences among the gender could be found. The next step would be a third wave study after graduation and with the start of the working life. It is assumed that the business life reality might act as an influence on the development of different roles in society for males and females.

5   Students' Attitude towards Entrepreneurship: Does Gender Matter?

5.1   Introduction

According to the Global Entrepreneurship Monitor (Sternberg & Lückgen, 2005) and the KfW Start-up Monitor 2005 (Hofmann et al., 2005) in Germany fewer women than men are interested in founding their own company (only 29%), although women represent half of the employed population.

Over the last twenty years, academics and economic organisations have demonstrated a growing interest in women entrepreneurs, especially in the United States and Canada where the number of women owned businesses has been rising. Female Entrepreneurship is now considered to be one of the sources of growth, employment, and innovation. In the United States, women owned businesses are the fastest growing sector of new ventures overall (Becker-Blease & Sohl, 2007). However, very little is known about women entrepreneurs (Orhan, 2001).

In contradiction to previous research, which concentrates on women and men during their professional activity, this study concentrates on an earlier point in time and that is before the working life begins: in the pre-start-up phase. This means that situational factors, for example unemployment or worse career opportunities, that could occur after the commencement of business activities have not been experienced yet and can not influence the selection of the professional career (self-employment or not). For this reason, students were selected as a target group; as in most cases students do not start their professional career during their studies. The micro-social environment (family background, friends, etc.), entrepreneurial education and specific cognitions (fostering and hindering perceptions) towards self employment that influence the professional choice remain and are examined in this study.

Thus, the goal of this study is to cover a variety of influences on founding intention (family background, educational environment, and cognition) analysed in regard to gender.

5.2   Literature Review

5.2.1 Gender Theory

The studies regarding gender-related differences can be assigned in general into two fundamental theories (Fischer et al., 1993). Liberal feminism as the first theory stems from the liberal political theory. Therein, it is argued that men and women are rational equal and do not differ in their capabilities and have, thus, the same potential in general. Observable rational differences between male and female entrepreneurs in their achievements are, hence, the result of certain kinds of discrimination during the socialisation. While men have the opportunity to realise their full potential, women are hindered to do so due to their socialisation. Liberal feminism concludes that if women are treated equally to men, the differences will diminish and women will be more like men. Social feminism is the second theory that serves as underlying base for research. Social feminism argues "that there are differences between males' and females' experiences from the earliest moments of life that result in fundamentally different ways of viewing the world" (Fischer et al., p. 154). As a result of this, men and women develop different traits which are, however, not unequal effective to pursue a goal. In contrast to the liberal feminism, the social feminism is seen as the more appropriate theory to explain gender-related differences (Fischer et al., 1993) and will therefore, serve within this chapter as base.

In literature that is based upon liberal feminism and on social feminism, there is no real consensus among scholars, whether small, large or if differences at all exist. Empirical findings seem to be diverse and in many cases contradictory. However, the field of female entrepreneurship and in extension gender differences in the founding behaviour and in the entrepreneurial behaviour has attracted some attention in the last twenty years (Sandberg, 2003; Mueller, 2004; Verheul & Thurik, 2001; Sexton & Bowman-Upton, 1990; Birley, 1989).

5.2.2 Male and Female Entrepreneurs

At the beginning, some well-known statements will be summarised for an introduction to the topic (Rosa et al., 1996; Verheul & Thurik, 2001):

- Female businesses under-perform in number of employees, sales turnover, etc.

- Female business owners are less likely to own multiple businesses, less eager to plan expansion and tend to start smaller businesses with a smaller amount of start-up capital than men.

- The value of assets in female businesses is significantly lower than in male businesses.

- Men are more likely to want to grow their own business as far as they can, while female entrepreneurs prefer working part-time and in the service sector.

- In comparison to men, women are more risk averse and spend less time on networking.

Thus, female and male entrepreneurs differ with respect to their personal and business profile: they start and run businesses in different sectors, develop different products, pursue different goals and structure their businesses in a different fashion (Brush, 1992; Fischer et al., 1993; Chaganti & Parasuraman, 1996; Carter et al., 1997; Verheul, 2003). Despite the mentioned economic importance of female entrepreneurs, their number still lags behind that of male entrepreneurs. According to Reynolds et al. (2002) men are about twice as likely to be involved in entrepreneurial activity as women and Minniti et al. (2005) show that in all countries participating in the Global Entrepreneurship Monitor in 2004 men are more active in entrepreneurship than women (Verheul et al., 2006).

Hence, men are more likely to be self-employed than women (Dolton & Makepeace, 1990). Entrepreneurial women are less likely then male entrepreneurs to be motivated by financial success and advancement, but by family and lifestyle (DeMartino & Barbato, 2003). Other studies emphasise the importance of independence, self-accomplishment and quality of life (Orhan, 2001; Bennett & Dann, 2000; Bradley & Boles, 2003). Especially need for independence plays an important role (Carter and Cannon, 1988). The three most important factors influencing women in becoming entrepreneurs are according to Ufuk and Oezgen (2001): meeting the family needs, initiating social relations, and self-fulfilment.

In contrast, financial gain is a strong motivation for males in general (Wilson et al., 2004), and less for women (Bradley & Boles, 2003). Similar conclusions are made by Ljunggren and Kolvereid (1996), who found that women are to perceive themselves as possessing higher entrepreneurial abilities than men do. Still, there is some evidence that women are less successful in these issues (Johnson & Storey, 1993) or at least often not taken as seriously as men are (Koper, 1993).

Besides the gender gap that is existent in venture creation and ownership activity, clear differences between the two genders exist as far as the founding setting is concerned. The fear of failure is more dominant to women as to men (Sternberg et al., 2004). Moreover, women are more likely to stress personal expectancies while men are more likely to stress economic expectancies during the start-up process of a firm (Ljunggren & Kolvereid, 1996).

Facing their personal situation, in general the probability of self-employment rises with age and number of children (Dolton & Makepeace, 1990). Furthermore, there is some evidence that women entrepreneurs tend to be older than their male counterparts (Johnson & Storey, 1993; Bennett & Dann, 2000). But, as Kolvereid (1996) argues, family background, gender, and self-employment experience only indirectly influence intentions to become self-employed through their effect on attitude, subjective norm and perceived behavioural control.

5.2.3 Business Foundation Intentions

An issue that should be stated is that most of the literature mentioned before focuses on differences or similarities between the two genders after the commencement of the business activities and that is during the start-up or the later phases of the corporate development. The pre-start-up phase seems to be neglected or at least it has not attracted the attention that it should have. There are several models that deal with the related corporate life cycle. These models vary from two stages (Dodge et al., 1994) to ten stages (Adizes, 1999). It is quite surprising that most of the models begin with the start-up phase and go on to the early development phase, but very few include the pre-start-up phase as a stage of the corporate development. However, it is in that particular phase that factors like personal intentions, motivation and family background etc. play the most important role in the employment status choice. The employment status choice has been defined by Katz (1992) as "the vocational decision process in terms of the individual's decision to enter an occupation as a wage-or-salaried individual or a self employed one" (p. 30).

Whereas research on entrepreneurship has been fostering the past years, there is a limited number of studies that focus on entrepreneurial intention among students. Wang and Wong (2004) concentrated on the level and the determinants of interest in entrepreneurship among university students in Singapore and have found among others that whereas students evaluated their business knowledge as poor, their interest to start-up a company is high. Scott and Twomey (1988) focused on university students' career aspiration in three countries, namely the USA, the U.K and Ireland, and found that the U.S sample aspiring to self-employment was low (25%) in comparison to the U.K. with 41% and Ireland with 34%. In a 1996 survey of 372 Norwegian business graduates, Kolvereid (1996) found that 38% preferred self-employment. Lüthje and Franke (2003) report that from a sample 2.193 engineering students, 44% indicate that they would quite probably and 11 % that they would very probably run their own company after the completion of their studies. From the interviewed students only a 3% were already self-employed.

According to Kourilsky and Walstad (1998), females are significantly less likely than males (62%-72%) to want to start their own business. Building on this and on the fact that there is indeed a gender gap in business ownership with more men being self employed than females, the first hypothesis is derived.

H1: The level of entrepreneurial intention is related to gender, males' intention is higher.

5.2.4 The Influence of Family Background

Sing and DeNoble (2003) found that personality, gender and having a close self-employed relative altogether have a strong positive relation to attitude on self-employment. In this context, Chen (1998) states that the number of entrepreneurial friends and relatives and the number of management courses were positive related to entrepreneurial decision and that male students expressed stronger intention toward becoming an entrepreneur than female students did.

In 1984, Klandt could show that the micro-social environment effects founding activity. This variable includes the family environment, i.e. where the person grew up as well as the family which he/she founded. Referring to Klandt (1984), the father's profession has an effect on the occupational decision of the son and the daughter, while the mother's influence is limited to the daughter. Thus, the father's profession seems to have a more universal influence. This study includes both the father's and the mother's self-employment as a further predictor of the personal goals and success perceptions of students.

Hence, there is some evidence, that children of entrepreneurs are more likely to found a company than others (Scott & Twomey, 1988; Wang & Wong, 2004). For example, a study from Benett and Dann (2000) indicates that almost half of the researched entrepreneurs had self-employed parents.

The present study investigates whether males with self-employed parents are more likely to be interested in founding their own business than females with the same family background. Going a step further it is differentiated between the influence of the father and the mother on the children's intention to become self employed.

H2: Males with self-employed parents are more likely to be interested in founding their own business than females with the same family background.

5.2.5 The Influence of the Educational Environment

Lee and Wong (2003) found that there is a positive relationship between entrepreneurship education and the intention to start a business. This was also found and confirmed by the study of Voigt et al. (2006) and Souitaris et al. (2007). In general, positive prior experience affects the perceptions of the desirability of starting a business (Peterman & Kennedy, 2003). A critical factor for successful entrepreneurship education is to include charismatic instructors who can communicate their enthusiasm for entrepreneurship through non-verbal expressiveness, because this will inspire students, which leads to a higher level of entrepreneurial intention. So the greater the inspiration from an entrepreneurship programme, the higher the students "post-programme" increase in attitude towards subjective norm and the intention to become self-employed (Souitaris et al., 2007).

Whereas in the USA entrepreneurial courses in higher education are offered since 1947 and there are chairs as early as the mid-60s, in Germany, the first chair of entrepreneurship was only established in 1997 at the European Business School (Klandt, 2006). Fortunately the situation in Germany is improving, as in 2006 there are more or less 60 professors specialised in the field (Klandt, 2006). This could be a step that would lead in a transition from an education that only prepares students to become employees or managers of large companies to an education that also prepares students or at least gives the knowledge of how to become self-employed.

Therefore the influence of the field of study, the chosen major, the entrepreneurial education on the founding intention will be investigated under the assumption that men posses a higher interest in becoming self-employed.

H3a: Males whose field of study is business administration have higher interest in becoming self-employed than females.

H3b: Males who have chosen entrepreneurship as their major have higher interest in becoming self-employed than females.

H3c: Males that have attended courses in entrepreneurship have higher interest in becoming self-employed than females.

5.2.6 Perceived Inhibiting (Hurdles) and Fostering (Motives) Factors towards the Founding Intention

Within the literature a plethora of studies can be found that analyses the perception of inhibiting and fostering factors of students (Möller, 1998; Görisch et al., 2002; Voigt et al., 2006; etc.). Möller (1998) found that the important founding reservations were the lack of start-up finance and the high degree of risk. Especially students with a low intention to start an own business saw those reasons as hindering factors. Furthermore, "Too much work and too little spare time" was named as an important hindering factor. The main distinction between students with a low interest in starting an own business and those who showed a medium to high interest was the missing business idea. Concerning the fostering factors, independence and a better opportunity for self-realisation were named as reasons to start an own business. Within the financial motives, the opportunity for profit was not as important as the financial reward for one's own initiative. Hence, it can be assumed that mainly inhibiting factors influence the founding intention. The results of Voigt et al. (2006) indicated as well that especially inhibiting factors seem to have the main impact on the founding intention.

Within the study of Görisch et al. (2002) only inhibiting factors were analysed. The main important inhibiting factor was the lack of start-up finance. Students with an interest in founding a business and those who would prefer an employment status differ in the motive of high personal risk as the latter perceived this factor as the second most problematic while for the former it played a minor role.

All studies have in common that fostering and inhibiting factors were not analysed in regard to the influence of gender. However, bearing in mind the basic assumption of the social feminism, that women differ fundamentally from men due to their socialisation, it is necessary to analyse how gender affects the influence of inhibiting and fostering factors on the founding intention. Therefore, the influence of inhibiting and fostering factors on the founding intention through the gender-lens will be investigated.

H4a: Inhibiting factors towards founding a company influence founding intention negatively. Gender differences in the perception of the factors are expected.

H4b: Fostering factors towards founding a company influence founding intention positively. Gender differences in the perception of the factors are expected.

5.3 Methodology

5.3.1 Research Methodology

The research process consisted of a four-step procedure which is orientated on an approach suggested by Kinnear and Taylor (1991). First, the identification and concretion of the research objective was done. Second, a written standardised questionnaire was compiled. Closed-ended questions were chosen, so that the respondents had to choose between the reply alternatives given (Schnell et al., 1995). Furthermore, the questionnaire was designed in a manner to fulfil necessary requirements regarding clarity, clearness and simplicity of the questions. Therefore, the structure of the questions was orientated on a procedure suggest by (1982) and Proctor (2000) which sees general and easy questions at the beginning and sensible or rather difficult questions at end of the questionnaire. Third, test interviews were conducted to improve the questionnaire. Therein, the debriefing method and the protocol method were used (Proctor, 2000). Test persons were students from the business faculty as well as senior research assistances from marketing and statistical chairs at the university. To ensure that also exchange students would be able to answer the questions, also non-German-native-speakers were members of the test group. The forth step was the data collection.

5.3.2 Operationalisation of Variables

Intention

In order to measure entrepreneurial intention, the validated scale by Klandt (1984) was applied. The question used was "Have you personally ever thought about founding your own business?". Possible answers are varying from 1 (=no, not yet), 2 (=yes, occasionally), 3 (=yes, relatively concrete) to 4 (=yes, I have made the decision to become self-employed).

Family Background

To measure the family background of the participants a scale of Möller (1998) was applied. "Manual, skilled or semi-skilled worker", "Salaried professional etc.", "Government employee", "Entrepreneur", "Freelancer or other self-employed" as well as "Other(s)" were given as answer alternatives.

Fostering and Inhibiting Factors

To measure the perception of fostering and inhibiting factors the scale of Möller (1998) was applied. Concerning the fostering factors the question was used "Please indicate which statement would best describe your feelings about starting a business" or respectively for the inhibiting factors "Please indicate which statement would best describe your feelings about NOT starting a business". Answer alternatives reached from 5 (=totally agree), 4 (=slightly agree), 3 (=neither...nor); 2 (=slightly disagree) to 1 (=totally disagree).

5.3.3 Data Collection and Sample Characteristics

The survey was conducted in winter 2006 at the Business School of the University of Erlangen-Nuremberg. The project was initiated and coordinated by the
University of Erlangen-Nuremberg in Nuremberg (Germany) and the European
Business School in Oestrich-Winkel (Germany). The questionnaire itself was
handed out to the students.

The sample of this study comprises 553 students from the Business School of
Nuremberg. The proportion of men and women is even. The average student is
23 years old, is in the fifth semester, single and has not attended entrepreneurship
lectures. Furthermore, the majority of almost 70% (67.5% male students and
68.9% female students) has chosen business administration as the major field of
study. Out of these, 44 students (28 male and 16 female) decided to focus on the
business start-up and entrepreneurship programme of the University of Erlangen-
Nuremberg. Looking at the family background, almost 26% of the male students
had a self-employed father and 12% a self-employed mother. In total the female
students showed more often an entrepreneurial family background, as almost
30% have a self-employed father and 16% a self-employed mother.

5.4   Results

The results will be presented in two parts. First, some descriptive findings will be
presented and then the focus will be on the findings from the hypothesis testing.

5.4.1 Descriptive Findings

The descriptives show that within this sample the founding intention is quite low
as more than half of the students, both male and female, thought only occasionally about founding a business (see table 24). If the mean score for the whole
sample is taken into consideration (AM: 1.1, SD: 1.01) then it can be stated that
there is almost no intention from the side of the student to become self-
employed.

Table 24: Have you personally ever thought about founding your own business

Founding Intentions	Percent	
	male	female
No. not yet	17.8	28.9
Yes. occasionally	55.8	57.0
Yes. relatively concrete	16.9	8.6
Yes. I have decided to become self employed	9.5	5.5
Total	**100**	**100.0**

Table 25 presents the mean and standard deviation results as far as the inhibiting variables are concerned. In all cases female students perceive the inhibiting variables more intimidating (preventing them from founding) than male students do.

Table 25: Please indicate which statement would best describe your feelings about NOT starting a business

Male		Inhibiting variables	Female	
AM	SD		AM	SD
2.65	1.29	Missing business knowledge	2.98	1.39
3.58	1.35	Missing concrete business idea	3.69	1.37
3.65	1.22	Missing seed capital	3.81	1.26
3.52	1.20	Insufficient practical experience	3.77	1.21
2.59	1.47	General missing interest	2.97	1.54
2.80	1.21	Missing founding partner /team	3.07	1.29
3.25	1.27	Missing business network	3.48	1.22
3.26	1.20	Missing market knowledge	3.42	1.25
3.02	1.09	Missing market transparency	3.18	1.16
2.10	1.30	Spouse or partner disapproves idea	2.13	1.26
3.66	1.71	High financial risk	3.90	1.09
2.84	1.15	Low income	3.06	1.18
2.90	1.81	Too much work for too less money	3.10	1.29
3.17	1.20	Too much work and too less spare-time	3.24	1.31
2.88	1.08	Bad economic climate	3.20	1.23
2.42	1.19	Bound to the own company	2.72	1.31
3.39	1.32	Risk of failure	3.63	1.25
2.19	1.08	Missing social appreciation	2.36	1.21

(5=totally agree to 1= totally disagree)

In Table 26 the mean and standard deviation results for the fostering variables are presented. In almost all cases female students perceive the fostering variables as more important for their founding intention than male students do.

Table 26: Please indicate which statement would best describe your feelings about starting a business

Male		Fostering variables	Female	
AM	SD		AM	SD
3.85	1.86	Self-realisation	4.11	0.93
4.06	1.11	Higher independency	4.11	0.92
3.29	1.21	Put studied into action	3.44	1.10
4.09	0.97	Higher autonomy of decision	4.13	0.88
2.85	1.73	Good economic climate	3.09	1.90
4.15	0.95	Realise idea/ Pursue own business idea	4.26	0.84
3.54	1.07	Gain experience	3.73	1.03
3.95	1.01	Bear responsibility	3.87	1.00
3.14	1.19	Higher prestige/ social status	3.07	1.09
3.66	1.16	Higher income	3.63	1.04
3.84	1.06	Potential profit	3.69	1.03
2.53	1.53	Continue family business	2.87	1.20
2.67	1.26	Motivation by friends and family	3.10	1.29

(5=totally agree to 1= totally disagree)

5.4.2 Hypotheses Testing

Hypothesis 1 stated that the level of entrepreneurial intention is related to gender and that males' intention is expected to be higher. The mean regarding the founding intention of male students is 1.28 (SD 1.063), for females is 0.96 (SD 0.932). The t-test (95%) showed significant differences in the founding intention between the genders (see table 27). Therefore hypothesis 1 is confirmed by the analysis of the data and this result is in accordance with recent research.

Table 27: t- Test, gender differences in the founding intention

	t	df	p
Intention	3.531	496	.000

n= 498, t= t value, df= degrees of freedom, p= significance at the 5% level

The second hypothesis and namely that males with self-employed parents are more likely to be interested in founding their own business than females with the same family background was only partially confirmed by the data. A t-test was conducted separately for the influence of the father's and the mother's self-employment on the founding intention of the children. Regarding the influence of the father (table 28), significant differences in the mean intention were found between male and female students (with males showing higher intention AM= 1.56 vs. AM= 1.12). However the same does not apply for the influence of the mother. No significant differences (table 29) could be found in the mean intention of males and females. Therefore the family background plays indeed a role in the formation of the entrepreneurial intention of the male and female students but the influence of the father is stronger than that of the mother.

Table 28: t-test, gender differences, influence of father's self-employment on founding intention

	t	df	p
Intention	1.981	116	.049

n= 118, t= t value, df= degrees of freedom, p= significance at the 5% level

Table 29: t-test, gender differences, influence of mother's self-employment on founding intention

		t	df	p
tion	Inten-	-0.323	66	.748

n= 68, t= t value, df= degrees of freedom, p= significance at the 5% level

As far as the influence of the education is concerned not all hypothesis are accepted. Hypothesis 3a on the field of study and entrepreneurial intention among males and females is accepted by the t-test analysis. Males whose field of study is business administration have higher interest in becoming self-employed than females (AM: 1.39 for male students vs. 1.02 for female students) and the difference is statistically significant (table 30). In testing hypothesis 3b, surprisingly the conducted t-test (table 31) showed no significant differences in the founding intentions of males and females that have chosen Entrepreneurship as a major. Thus, this hypothesis is rejected by the data of this study. Once more surprisingly the conducted t-test (table 32) showed no significant differences in the founding intentions of males and females who had attended courses in entrepreneurship. Male students however seem to have a slightly higher intention to become self employed than female students after they attended courses in Entrepreneurship (AM: 1.45 for male students vs. 1.33 for female students). Hence, also this hypothesis can not be confirmed in this study.

Table 30: t- Test, gender differences, influence of field of study on founding intention

		t	df	p
tion	Inten-	3.240	334	.001

n= 336, t= t value, df= degrees of freedom, p= significance at the 5% level

Table 31: t- Test, gender differences, influence of major on founding intention

	t	df	p
Inten-tion	1.878	36	.68

n= 38, t= t value, df= degrees of freedom, p= significance at the 5% level

Table 32: t- Test, gender differences, influence of courses in entrepreneurship on founding intention

	t	df	p
Intention	-0.656	105	.514

n= 104, t= t value, df= degrees of freedom, p= significance at the 5% level

As previously already stated various fostering and inhibiting variables towards entrepreneurship were taken into consideration for this study. A confirmatory factor analysis (varimax rotation, main component analysis) reduced the 18 different inhibiting variables into four factors. These are: lack of pre start-up know-how, financial and failure risks, lack of interest and ideas, social hindrances. The four factors together explain a total of 57.57 percent of the variance. The first factor includes items like little market knowledge, no partner, and no practical experience and explains 35.19 percent of the variance. In the financial and failure risk factor the fear of large financial risk, too much work and the fear of failure are included (9.18 percent of the variance). The third factor includes no interest and no ideas (7.87 percent of the variance). Finally the social hindrances are no family support and no prestige (5.33 percent of the variance).

The correlation analysis (Table 33) for the whole sample (both male and female students) shows that there is a negative relationship between all the inhibiting factors and the founding intention. In other words the stronger the inhibiting factors are perceived the lower becomes the intention to become self-employed. The correlation between intention and the social hindrance factor is quite low (-.092) but still negative and significant at the 5% significance level. These results confirm the first part of the hypothesis 4a.

Table 33: Correlation analysis, intention and hindering factors

		lack of know-how	financial and fail-ure risk	lack of interest	social hin-drances
Intention	Correlation Pearson	-.164(**)	-.217(**)	-.214(**)	-.092(*)
	Significance (2-sided)	.000	.000	.000	.043
	n	483	480	482	480

** The correlation is at the level 0.01 (2-sided) significant.* The correlation is at the level 0.05 (2-sided) significant.

To test whether differences in the perception of the hindering factors between the two gender exist, two separate linear regression analyses for the male and female sample were conducted (the exact results of the regression analysis can be found in the appendices). As independent variables the four inhibiting factors have been used with the founding intention as dependent variable. For the male sample only the lack of interest factor was significant (beta value= -0.162) and all the factors explain 5.3% of the variance in intention. The regression analysis for the women sample shows that the financial risk factor is the only significant influence (beta value= -0.225). Here almost 8% of intention variance is explained (R^2).

In the case of the fostering variables once more a confirmatory factor analysis (with four factors, varimax rotation, and main component analysis) has been conducted. The 13 fostering factors were reduced to four factors and namely: independence, status, external factors and experience. The four factors explain 66.89 percent of the variance. The independence factor includes striving for in-dependence and freedom in decision making and explains 34.77 percent of the variance. The status factors includes items like higher prestige, higher income (14.07 percent of the variance). External factors are motivation by family and friends as well as good market conditions (11.02 percent of the variance). Finally the experience factor consists of the variables making one's own experience and putting knowledge into practice.

The correlation analysis (table 34) for the whole sample (both male and female students) shows that there is a positive relationship between three fostering factors and the founding intention. This means that the stronger the fostering factors are perceived the higher becomes the intention to become self-employed. The correlation between intention and external factors is not significant. These results partially confirm the first part of the hypothesis 4b.

Table 34: Correlation analysis, intention and fostering factors

		independence	status	external	experience
intention	Correlation Pearson	.248(**)	.117(*)	.086	.180(**)
	Significance (2-sided)	.000	.010	.059	.000
	n	484	483	483	484

** The correlation is at the level 0.01 (2-sided) significant.* The correlation is at the level 0.05 (2-sided) significant.

Once more two separate linear regression analyses has been conducted for the female and the male sample, to test whether differences in the perception of the hindering factors between the two gender exist (the exact results of the regression analysis can be found in the appendices). Regarding the male group, all the factors explain approximately 9% of the variance, whereas only the independence factor is significant (beta value= 0.245). As far as women are concerned, all the fostering factors explain around 6% of the variance of the founding intention. Here as well only the independence factor is significant (beta value= 0.163).

5.5   Discussion and Conclusion

The comparison in the founding intention between males and females showed significant differences. This result confirms the conventional wisdom that the entrepreneurial intention of males is higher than those of females (e.g. Kourilsky & Walstad, 1998; Wang & Wong, 2004; Möller, 1998). It is therefore not only the founding activity of men higher but the founding intention as well.

In the sample the family background showed only partially a significant influence on founding intention, however, with the father's influence resulting only in significant differences in the founding intention of male and female students. So, the second hypothesis is only partially supported.

Also, the third hypothesis (H3a, H3b, and H3c) which deals with study-related factors could only partly proved by this sample. When only looking at the field of study, males were more interested in founding one's own business than women. The findings tend to indicate that there could be a positive relationship between general business administration education and the intention to start a business. Surprisingly entrepreneurship as major and courses in entrepreneurship did not bring significant differences in the founding intention of the two genders. Perhaps this is because the sub-sample that has chosen entrepreneurship as a major is quite low in number.

Hypothesis 4a assumed that inhibiting factors towards founding a company influence founding intention negatively. This part of the hypothesis is supported from the data. The second part of the hypothesis was only partially confirmed. The lack of interest factor was found significant only for men. The financial and failure risk was found significant only for women. Hence, females perceive the establishment of a new company as more risky (especially financial risk) than men. This is in accordance with the results of recent literature (e.g. Johnson & Storey, 1993; Voigt et al., 2006; Ljunggren & Kolvereid, 1996; Sternberg et al., 2004).

Hypothesis H4b stated that fostering factors towards founding a company influence founding intention positively. This part of the hypothesis is accepted. When making the gender comparison for both groups only the independence factor is significant. Thus, the results are surprising, as men are generally supposed to be strongly focused by financial gain (Wilson et al., 2004; Bradley & Boles, 2003). However the results show that men and women differ according to inhibiting factors but not regarding to fostering factors. Therefore the gender gap regarding the perception of a potential venture creation can only be partly supported.

5.6   Implications for Entrepreneurship Research and Practice

The research on German students with a focus on gender differences as far as founding a company is concerned should help in understanding the emergence of differences in the German founding landscape and in deducing recommendations for action. Furthermore this research should help us understand gender-related differences in founding intentions due to perception of various fostering and inhibiting factors.

As people before entrance into the working life were examined, influences of the working life can be controlled partially (not to 100%). As the measurement already takes place at an early point in time (during the studies), it can be intervened in time, in order to finally strengthen the interest of founding a company and also the founding activity of women.

The results of the study could also have important implications for the academic field. The result that student's intention to become self-employed is very low should serve a starting point for academics to rebuild entrepreneurship education. Adjusting the support activities and the lecture contents in a way that awakes the entrepreneurial interest for both male and female students is of great importance. In addition it seems that mostly women are lacking information about financial support when planning to found a business. This could be included in lectures, too.

5.7　　Limitation – Suggestions for Further Research

The selection of a single country has the obvious limitation of the generalisability of the results across populations and geographical settings. Furthermore, the limitation in generalisability also arises from the fact that the research took place in a specific time period, giving us a snapshot of the situation at a particular point in time. The results found, may not be applicable if the circumstances change. In addition, the survey was conducted at only one University, which could affect the explanatory content.

Of course intention can predict activity but it is not activity itself. In a further step a longitudinal study could enable a further look to whether students' intention to become self-employed has become realisation and if not why. If on the other hand intention has become activity it is important to see the quality (in terms of turn over, number of employees, self realisation of the founder, etc.) of the start ups founded by former students.

6 Entrepreneurship Education in the United Kingdom and Germany

6.1 Introduction

In general entrepreneurship education has the basic assumption that the competencies of an entrepreneur can be learned (Kulicke, 2006). This assumption is as well supported as it is doubted within the scientific literature and research. For example, the former researcher of the Massachusetts Institute of Technology, David L. Birch, who laid a milestone in entrepreneurship in the late seventies by stating that 82% of all new ventures are created by small businesses, argued in an interview in the Academy of Management Learning and Education in 2004 that it is not possible to teach people to be entrepreneurs (Aronsson, 2004). Drucker (1985) on the other hand states that entrepreneurship is a process and can be learned and is, thus, teachable. Ronstadt (1987) points out, in addition, that "strong indications exist that 'entrepreneurship education' will produce more and better entrepreneurs" (p. 37). The positive effect of entrepreneurship education on entrepreneurial behaviour and activity was found by researchers such as Lee (2003), Webb et al. (1982) and Voigt et al. (2006).

Entrepreneurship education is, however, not just restricted to the educational programme that provides necessary business know-how but also to the creation of an entrepreneurial climate and culture that motivates students to become self-employed (e.g. Klofsten, 2000; Kulicke, 2006). State-initiated programmes like the German EXIST and the UK SEC that supports university programmes financially have, not only the aim to support necessary knowledge transfer but to raise the awareness of entrepreneurial activity in a scientific environment (EXIST, 2007). Even if university entrepreneurship education has attracted a great deal of attention in scientific research (e.g. Peterman/Kennedy, 2003; Young, 1997; Klandt, 2004; Gorman, et al., 1997), there is clearly more than just one successful concept of entrepreneurship education, in particular within universities (Matlay, 2006). The study of six entrepreneurship programmes of Garavan and O'Cinneide (1994) emphasise that it is more important that the entrepreneurship programme has to be specifically orientated towards the target population.

Furthermore, existing studies have generally taken a single-country approach to analyse the intention or the determinants of student entrepreneurial activity and

the effect of entrepreneurial education (e.g. Wang & Wong, 2004; Singh & De-
Noble, 2003; Dolton & Makepeace, 1990; Tkachev & Kolvereid, 1999; Voigt et
al., 2006). An exception to this is illustrated by Hytti and Gorman (2004) who
compared entrepreneurship education methods in four countries.

In this chapter the entrepreneurial programme of the German Friedrich-
Alexander-University of Erlangen-Nuremberg and the Metropolitan University
of Leeds will be compared by means of a survey. In doing so students who have
and who have not attended entrepreneurship lectures were included into the survey sample so that the effect of entrepreneurship education can, thus, be examined on those students whose knowledge and perception has been influenced directly by the academic programme. By including students who have no previous
knowledge acquired by entrepreneurship lectures and/or courses, it is possible to
examine the general intention of students to start or found a company and the
indirect effect of an entrepreneurial climate and culture towards the perception of
factors that may either foster or inhibit individuals from starting their own business, or being entrepreneurial.

6.2   Entrepreneurship Education in Germany and the United Kingdom

For several decades, there has been a rapid growth in the number of professorships, academic organisations, journals and other publications, especially in the
United States, in the area of entrepreneurship and entrepreneurship-related matters (Robinson, 1991). In comparison with other disciplines in the field of business administration and economics, entrepreneurship is a relatively young and
emerging subject. While in the United States, the focus is on theory, case studies
and lectures, in Europe the majority of programmes a more practical, with an ex-
periential teaching approach that can generally be observed.

However, even within Europe, there is a heterogeneous situation. While the
United Kingdom, Spain and the Netherlands offer a relatively broad range of activities, there is almost no incentive for entrepreneurial education in Italy and
France, while German, Austrian and Swiss institutions have made noteworthy
efforts in order to establish entrepreneurship education at many universities.
Nevertheless, the first chair of entrepreneurship in Germany was established in
1997 (Klandt, 2005) and since then, there have been a growing number of entrepreneurship professorships, now totalling approximately 56 (Moog, 2005). How-

ever, it is argued that there is still a need for improvement, especially for the long term strategy and economic benefits alluded to earlier in this paper (Moog, 2005).

Although many universities are offering an entrepreneurship education programmes and the number is still growing, no common approach exists as to how to educate entrepreneurs efficiently and effectively. A basic approach is to understand the term entrepreneurship as learning about entrepreneurship as a phenomenon and learning useful skills in order to become an entrepreneur (Rasmussen & Sørheim, 2006). In order to stimulate this entrepreneurship by study programmes, Klofsten (2000) argues that three basic activities should be taken into consideration:

- Creation and maintenance of an entrepreneurship culture throughout all university activities

- Courses in entrepreneurship with the focus on theoretical issues like start-up financing etc.

- Specific training programmes to support individuals who wish to start their own business

To fulfil these requirements, a clear view on the aspects of an entrepreneur is needed. Lazear (2000) defines entrepreneurs as "individuals who are multi-faceted. Although not necessarily superb at anything, entrepreneurs have to be sufficiently skilled in a variety of areas to put together the many ingredients required to create a successful business. As a result, entrepreneurs tend to be more balanced individuals" (Lazear, 2000, p. 34). Kirschbaum argues (1990) that the aim of entrepreneurship education is to create a generalist more than a specialist. This can be done by focusing on a broad educational programme which addresses the relevant aspects of starting a new business in theory and practice (Klofsten, 2000). Common instruments are seminars, business games and business plan competitions (Winand & Nathusius, 1990). Another important factor is to integrate external experts such as successful entrepreneurs (Hopkins & Feldman 1989).

These views are echoed by Gibb (2006) who also argues for a holistic approach to entrepreneurship education described as a "optimum fully integrated model" featuring university wide entrepreneurship teaching, innovative pedagogical sup-

port, interdisciplinary teaching joined with technology transfer and opportunity
to develop intellectual property (for staff and students) among other features. The
aim is to develop an entrepreneurial mindset featuring a number of key behaviours, attributes and skills such as opportunity seeking, initiative, creativity, self-
confidence, perseverance, networking, judgment and selling.

The study cooperation "Business Start-up and Entrepreneurship" at the Friedrich-
Alexander-University Erlangen-Nuremberg and the courses from The Institute
for Enterprise at Leeds Metropolitan University such as "Business Creation and
Enterprise" and "International Enterprise" illustrate such approaches, which will
be described within this chapter.

6.3   Entrepreneurship Education Concepts

At the University of Erlangen-Nuremberg, the approach of a 'study-cooperation'
was initiated in 2001. The goal is to use the wide scope of existing different education aspects and the competence of different chairs combined with a central
coordination unit. The concept is supplemented with additional education elements, in order to form a generalist entrepreneur. The advantage is to keep the
bureaucratic costs relatively low while offering a high level of qualitative education.

At Leeds Metropolitan University a two pronged approach has been adopted. It
could be argued that this approach roughly divides into taught modules of a
modular degree programme that are mainly 'about entrepreneurship' that is they
are theoretically based using case studies and lectures etc. The second branch is
to offer students extra-curricular business start-up education in the form of workshops, summer school, one to one advice etc. which has been conceived partly in
response to the results of the entrepreneurial intentions survey carried out over a
number of years at Leeds Metropolitan University. This second branch is firmly
in the 'for entrepreneurship' category, offering practical advice and support to
those wanting to start a business or social enterprise. More recently, the Institute
for Enterprise has helped to develop courses that span both campuses, being simultaneously 'for' and 'about' entrepreneurship.

6.3.1 Entrepreneurship Education at the University of Erlangen-Nuremberg

The Faculty of Economics and Social Sciences is the biggest institution within the Friedrich-Alexander-University Erlangen-Nuremberg. With approximately 5,000 students and 35 chairs the faculty is one of the largest in southern Germany. The wide range of teaching consists of over 50 courses of study and is strongly influenced by the inter-disciplinary cooperation with other faculties and external institutions.

In 2000, the Faculty of Business Administration and Economics decided to offer a study programme with emphasis on entrepreneurship and starting a business. After comparisons of possible models a study cooperation concept was chosen which was named "Unternehmensgründung & Entrepreneurship" ("Business Start-up and Entrepreneurship"). Hence, the competence of the existing 35 chairs could be pooled for the entrepreneurship education by integrating their specific knowledge in a variety of lectures, seminars and events. It is also essential that the scope for the development of students' own business ideas within the programme exists.

The study cooperation concept is composed of three columns. The first column represents the lectures and seminars offered. Students can major in entrepreneurship, in which every student has to attend a core programme consisting of seven lectures and seminars (Theory and Process of Entrepreneurship, Business Plan Seminar, Start-Up Financing, Quantitative Management Techniques, Legal Identity and Taxation, Foundation and Development of Technology Companies). The key course is the business plan seminar in which students work in teams to write a business plan for a business proposal of their choice.

In addition, students have to choose from disciplines dealing with e-business, logistics, marketing, national and international accounting, cost calculation and accounting, controlling, law, business management, organisational and social psychology, auditing, mobile engineering as well as management and international management. It can be seen that dependent on the specific interest and needs of the student, diverse combinations are possible from over 35 lectures or seminars. Furthermore, excellent students have the chance to apply for an international entrepreneurship camp which is held once a year at locations such as Boston University and the Tongji University in Shanghai. At the end of the programme, each student must submit a master thesis with a clear focus on start-up, entrepreneurship and/or innovation management.

The study cooperation furthermore integrates, as second column, practitioners, entrepreneurs and experts in entrepreneurship education to enable the students to gain from their practical knowledge and experience. Hopkins and Feldman (1989) argue in this context that this approach can improve the entrepreneurship education substantially. The seminar "Start-Up Financing" for example is held by an external professional expert from a bank, who is responsible for the department "New Venture Foundation and Seed Financing". A business angel gives the lecture "Foundation and Development of Technology Companies". They also support business ideas from students in the realisation process and whilst on the business plan seminar, successful entrepreneurs are invited to teach students how to write a 'real' business plan.

The third and final column exists to create an effective networking platform to forge links between students with business ideas and incubators or other supporting organisations. Students are, for example, encouraged to take part in an inter-disciplinary business plan competition which is organised by the organisation "Netzwerk Nordbayern" [Network Northern Bavaria] and in order to further create a useful network between the entrepreneurship students an online alumni forum was established to offer students job vacancies, internships and field reports. Finally, in a parallel effort to bring the idea of starting a business and entrepreneurship into schools, there is an initiative called 'Entrepreneur of Tomorrow' which focuses on pupils in their last school year before taking A-level examinations.

Summer 2001 saw the first cohort of students offered the choice of the new study cooperative. The first intake was about 20 participating students, which has since risen to approximately 70 students currently studying entrepreneurship.

6.3.2 Entrepreneurship Education at Leeds Metropolitan University

Leeds Metropolitan University has been at the forefront of entrepreneurship education in the UK for a number of years with initiatives such as Business Start-Up and, more recently, The Institute for Enterprise. 'Enterprise', in the context of generic skills development, has been adopted as a core learning theme across undergraduate provision in each of the Faculties of the University. Leeds Business

School was the original focus of enterprise teaching, having run small business modules at Level 2 since 1985 and entrepreneurial studies modules at level 3 since 1988. Since then, enterprise modules have been developed and delivered across a wide range of 'non-business' areas. For example such modules have been included in degrees in Events Management, Hospitality and Retail Management, Sport and Leisure, Computing, Multi-Media and Music and Health Sciences.

Enterprise modules are now offered on both Further and Higher Education programmes and currently there are over 1,500 students across the University each year studying modules which encourage innovation, creativity and enterprise. Taster sessions and personal development programmes are run within other degrees as diverse as Graphic Art and Design, Fine Art, Business Studies and the Built Environment.

However, the University recognises that there are many barriers to graduate entrepreneurship that is, the creation and management of a new organisation. This is reflected in an annual survey of over 3,500 students across four West Yorkshire Universities (Robertson, 2004-6). In general terms the surveys found that:

• 4% of the students surveyed were currently engaged in entrepreneurial activity whilst completing their education;

• 50% indicated that they will definitely or probably enter self employment at some stage post graduation;

• 44% intended to enter self employment within 5 years of graduation;

• 23% of the students surveyed felt that they did not have the skills to start-up a business;

• 39% expected help from the university to start-up their business.

In recognition of these factors Leeds Metropolitan University, through the Business Start-Up programme, provides a variety of business support offerings which are on the whole, extra-curricular. These include workshops, access to a resident business advisor, annual business concept competition, an entrepreneurial summer school, proof of concept funding, networking events and pre-start incubation space. The University also provides a 'Business Incubator' which offers managed office space and intensive support for businesses less than three years old.

Building on the success of this programme, the University was awarded funding to establish The Institute for Enterprise, as a Centre for Excellence in 2005 to facilitate curriculum development, assessment, learning and teaching, and enterprise education across the whole University building on established practice. For the Business School, who participated in the survey carried out for this research paper, this has meant the establishment of two new awards. The first is Business Creation and Enterprise, a one-year programme at Level 3 offering students the opportunity to both theorise and practice business start-up, drawing together the resources of the Business School, Business Incubator and Business Start-Up. The award includes modules such as Business Strategy, SMEs Environmental Context, Business Enterprise Operations, Growth & Strategic Planning, Sales & Customer Relationship Management, Consultancy Project and Personal, Academic and Career Effectiveness. Finally this course also includes a semester within the Leeds Met Incubator, with full access to office facilities and the programme of business support, during which students gain academic credit for and while pursuing their business and social enterprise ideas. The second new award is a Masters programme in International Enterprise to enhance students' careers in business growth and development by focussing on small, medium and/or family owned businesses with aspirations for international development. In this course students undertake four core modules of Entrepreneurship, Strategic Management of International Enterprises, International Marketing and International Finance culminating in the enterprise project that requires students to undertake a substantive piece of individual work based upon entrepreneurial aspects with potential for international application.

Other examples of enterprise education exist within the various faculties of the University, notably the Leslie Silver International Faculty offering courses in Tourism, Hospitality & Events where similar thinking has brought about courses that are both 'for' and 'about' entrepreneurship and enterprise education in general. These and other similar initiatives have increased the overall enterprise and entrepreneurship content on offer within the University, and especially the Business School, both intra- and extra-curricular, and it is the purpose of this research study to determine whether these initiative are having the desired impact on the student cohort.

6.4   Methodology

6.4.1 Questionnaire

The research process consisted of a four step procedure which is orientated on an approach suggested by Kinnear and Taylor (1991). First, the identification of the research objectives with the hypotheses were established. Second, a written standardised questionnaire was compiled in German and translated into English. Hence, all participants had the same questions in the same order and with the same wording, in both languages (Schnell et al., 1995). Closed-ended questions were chosen, so that the respondents had to choose between reply alternatives given (Schnell et al., 1995). Therein, a verbal scale rating to answers was used. Furthermore, the questionnaire was designed in a manner to fulfil requirements such as clarity, clearness and simplicity of the questions. A special focus was on the multi-level proof-reading by native speakers of both languages at all development stages of the questionnaire to ensure clarity and comparability. Therefore, the questions were firstly translated from German into English, and then the questionnaire was revised by native speakers, as well as the appropriate German version. Finally, test interviews were conducted to improve the questionnaire. Test persons were students from the business faculty as well as senior research assistants from the Marketing and Statistical departments at the University of Erlangen-Nuremberg and Leeds Metropolitan University. The surveys in Germany and UK were conducted in between November 2006 and March 2007.

6.4.2 Operationalisation

To measure the perception of fostering and inhibiting factors a scale of Möller (1998) was applied. The fostering factors were analysed with the question "Please indicate which statement would best describe your feelings about starting a business" or respectively for the inhibiting factors "Please indicate which statement would best describe your feeling about NOT starting a business". Answer alternatives ranged from 5 (–totally agree), 4 (=slightly agree), 3 (=neither...nor), 2 (=slightly disagree) to 1 (totally disagree). Within the questionnaire 13 fostering questions were included (see Table 35).

Table 35: Fostering factors

Self-realisation	Bear responsibility
Higher independency	Higher prestige/social status
Put studies into action	Higher income
Higher autonomy of decision	Potential profit
Good economic climate	Continue family business
Realise idea/Pursue own business idea	Motivation by friends and family
Gain experience	

As regards the inhibiting factors 18 questions were provided as factors rated by the respondents (see Table 36).

Table 36: Inhibiting factors

Missing business knowledge	Spouse or partner disapproves idea
Missing concrete business idea	High financial risk
Missing seed capital	Low income
Insufficient practical experience	Too much work for too less money
General missing interest	Too much work and too less spare-time
Missing founding partner /team	Bad economic climate
Missing business network	Bound to the own company
Missing market knowledge	Risk of failure
Missing market transparency	Missing social appreciation

A validated scale by Klandt (1984) was applied to measure the founding intentions among students. The question used was "Have you personally ever thought about founding your own business?". Possible answers varied on a range from 1 (=no, not yet), 2 (=yes, occasionally), 3 (=yes, relatively concrete) to 4 (=yes, I have made the decision to become self-employed).

6.5   Research Questions

The origins of the suggested hypotheses emanates from the research focus on students within two separate universities and in relation to the numerous studies concerning the analysis of the perception of fostering and inhibiting factors of students (Möller, 1998; Görisch et al., 2002; Voigt et al., 2006). Möller (1998) for example found that the important founding reservations were the "lack of start-up finance" and the "high degree of risk". In particular, students with a low intention to start an own business saw those reasons as hindering factors. Furthermore, "too much work and too little spare time" was named as an important hindering factor. The main distinction between students with a low interest in starting their own business and those who showed a medium to high interest was the lack of a suitable business idea. The fostering factors, "independence" and a better "opportunity for self-realisation" were named as reasons to start a business. As regards the financial motives, the "opportunity for profit" was not as important as the "financial reward" for using ones own initiative. In contrast to the inhibiting factors, however, it was not mentioned in this study any difference between students according to their founding intention. Hence, it can be assumed, more often than not that inhibiting factors influence the intention to start a business The study results of Voigt et al. (2006) confirmed that in particular inhibiting factors seem to have the main impact on this intention.

Such studies are becoming an increasingly important area of the study of entrepreneurial intentions because they offer an insight and deeper understanding into the perceptions of students with regards to founding a business. Lüthje and Franke (2003) claim that entrepreneurial intent is directly affected by perceived fostering and inhibiting factors in the entrepreneurship-related context. Fostering factors might encourage, promote and influence or inspire students to want to start a business. Inhibiting factors likewise might discourage, dissuade or oppose them to want to start a business.

Therefore, in light of the two country samples comparative results will be provided to examine whether students in the UK and Germany perceive fostering and inhibiting factors differently. Firstly all participating students at the University of Erlangen-Nuremberg and the Leeds Metropolitan University will be compared and then only those students will be examined who have already attended entrepreneurship lectures and/or courses. The effect of entrepreneurship education can, thus, be examined on those students whose knowledge and perception was already influenced by the academic curriculum. In addition, by including students who have no previous knowledge acquired by entrepreneurship lectures and/or courses, it is possible to examine the general founding or start-up intention of students at the University of Erlangen-Nuremberg and Leeds Metropolitan University and the indirect effect of an arguably entrepreneurial climate and culture towards the perception of fostering and inhibiting factors

Therefore following research questions are proposed:

Research question 1: Do students in the UK and Germany perceive fostering factors differently?

Research question 2: Do students in the UK and German, who have attended entrepreneurship lectures/courses, perceive fostering factors differently?

Research question 3: Do students in the UK and Germany perceive inhibiting factors differently?

Research question 4: Do students in the UK and German, who have attended entrepreneurship lectures/courses, perceive inhibiting factors differently?

According to the GEM-country report Germany 2006 (Sternberg et al., 2007) the percentage of entrepreneurial activity is higher in the UK than in Germany. While the total of early entrepreneurial activity was in 2006 5.8% in the UK, the percentage in Germany was 4.2% (Harding, 2007). Even the general attitude towards starting a business is better in the UK than in Germany. In the UK 7.8% stated that they expect to start a business in the next three years while in Germany only 6.7% agreed with this statement. Hence, it is interesting to analyse whether this entrepreneurial difference and gap between the UK and Germany can be identified at an earlier point of time, in this case while attending University. The results could offer an explanation whether the difference already exists or if it is developed during the period of higher education or at the commencement of the working life. Therefore, following research question was proposed:

Research question 5: Do UK students differ in their intention to start a business from German students?

Lee and Wong (2003) found that there is a positive relationship between entrepreneurship education and the intention to start a business. Lüthje and Franke also state in their 2003 paper that courses in entrepreneurship and the image of business founders within the university encourage graduates to become self-employed. Therefore, it will be investigated whether the students who have attended the entrepreneurship programme differ in their intention to start a business.

Research question 6: Do students from UK and Germany, who have attended entrepreneurship lectures/courses, differ in the intention to found a business?

Figure 23 summarises the proposed research questions and the given theoretical framework.Figure 23: Research framework

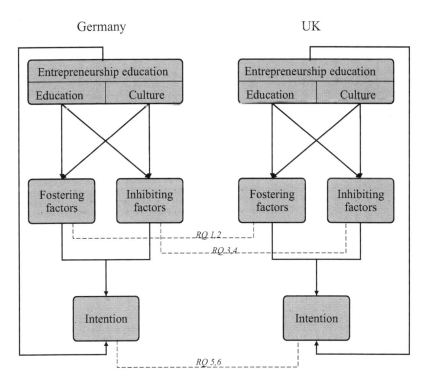

6.6   Descriptive Findings

Overall 747 students participated in both countries with 553 questionnaires completed in Germany and 194 in the UK. While the majority of students in Germany (302) were already in their major period of study, all responding students from Leeds were still in their bachelor study period (levels 1-3). The proportion of students who had attended entrepreneurship classes at this date were 122 within the German sub-sample and 42 in the UK sub-sample. The imbalance can be explained by the different entrepreneurship education and study programmes. While German students have to choose an entrepreneurship lecture or seminar, the content is often automatically included into the study programme of the Leeds Metropolitan University.

Equal numbers of male and female students (275) participated at the Friedrich-Alexander-University of Erlangen-Nuremberg, while in Leeds the quota of male respondents was 104 and female 90 students The average student from the Friedrich-Alexander-University (FAU) of Erlangen-Nuremberg was 23 years old and had Business Administration as field of study (see figure 24). The average student from the Metropolitan University of Leeds was 22 years old and was studying Business Studies (see figure 25). More than half of the German and 30 percent of the UK students did not start their studies directly after finishing school. An apprenticeship illustrates the main reason for this with 34% of the German students, but only 3% of the UK students, completed an apprenticeship or similar UK equivalent (an initial period training within an organisation).

Figure 24: Major fields of study (FAU Erlangen-Nuremberg)

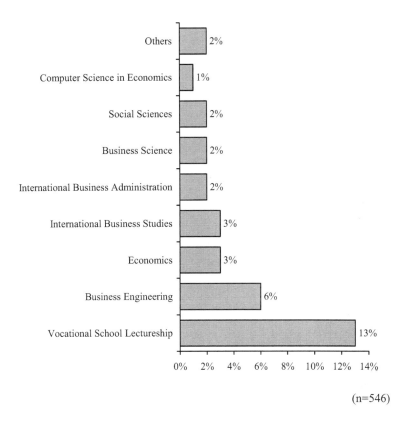

(n=546)

Figure 25: Major fields of study (Leeds Metropolitan University)

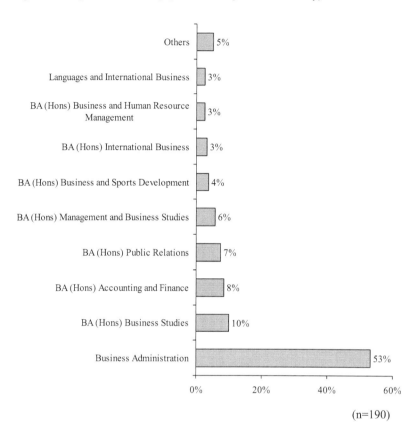

(n=190)

The founding intention within the sample is relatively high as, only 21.2 percent of the German and 29.8 percent of the English students see self-employment as not an alternative for their personal career choice (see table 36).

Table 36: Do you wish to start your own business?

| German sample | | | UK sample | |
Frequency	Valid Percent	Founding Intentions	Frequency	Valid Percent
117	21.2	No.	58	29.8
282	51.2	Yes. I do but I do not yet have a specific idea.	105	54.1
63	11.4	Yes. I do and I have a strong idea.	20	10.3
21	3.8	Yes. I did but I abandoned it at the "idea" stage.	3	1.6
37	6.7	Yes. I do and I already have precise plans.	3	1.6
10	1.8	Yes. I do and I am in the process of starting up.	1	0.5
19	3.5	Yes. I currently run my own business	3	1.6
2	0.4	Yes. I have run my own business in the past, but not anymore.	1	0.5
551	100	Total	194	100

Looking at micro-social influences in the sample it was found that 27.3% of the German students had a self-employed father and another 14.3% a self-employed mother. The UK students showed almost the same entrepreneurial family background, as almost 26.1% have a self-employed father and 14.0% a self-employed mother (see table 37).

Table 37: Parents' occupation

German sample		Father's Occupation	UK sample	
Frequency	Valid Percent		Frequency	Valid Percent
62	12.8	Manual. skilled or semi-skilled worker	43	22.9
180	37.3	Salaried professional. administrative etc.	52	27.6
84	17.4	Government employee	14	7.4
98	20.3	Entrepreneur	18	9.6
34	7.0	Freelancer or other self-employed	31	16.5
12	2.5	Other(s)	19	10.1
13	2.7	No answer	11	5.9
483	100	N	188	100

German sample		Mother's Occupation	UK sample	
30	5.6	Manual. skilled or semi-skilled worker	16	8.3
242	45.0	Salaried professional. administrative etc.	67	34.9
77	14.3	Government employee	24	12.5
59	11.0	Entrepreneur	7	3.7
18	3.3	Freelancer or other self-employed	20	10.4
108	20.1	Other(s)	48	25.0
4	0.7	No answer	10	5.2
538	100	N	192	100

22% of all students had previous experience of courses in entrepreneurship or business start-up modules, lectures, workshops or summer schools (see table 38).

Table 38: Undertaking of entrepreneurial courses

German sample		Undertaking of entrepreneurial courses	UK sample	
Frequency	Valid Percent		Frequency	Valid Percent
123	23.1	Yes	42	22.3
409	76.9	No	146	77.7
532	100	N	188	100

6.7   Empirical Analysis

All the hypotheses were tested on a 5% significance level. In addition, a Levene-test was conducted to examine whether both independent samples possess the same variance. In case of a same variance, a t-test for independent samples with a same variance was used for the analysis. Following this, the hypotheses regarding the perception of fostering and inhibiting factors as well as the intention to found a business is then described. Therein, the hypotheses will be tested for all students from UK and Germany and for those who have attended lectures or courses in entrepreneurship.

6.7.1   Comparison of all Students

6.7.1.1 Comparison of Fostering Factors

Within the study nine fostering factors are perceived significantly different of students from the UK and Germany (see table 39). Hence, the research question 1 is partially supported.

Both student groups see self-employment as a possibility to achieve a higher degree of independence, but UK students tend to rate this aspect higher. However, the difference between the student groups, with respect to the confidence interval of the mean value difference (-0.324 - 0.027), is only small. The confidence interval for the mean value has the lower limit (LL) of-0.324 and the upper limit of (-0.027). The confidence interval indicates with a probability of 95% that the difference between the both mean values is between -0.0324 and -0.0027. The negative algebraic sign shows that the first sub-sample has a lower mean value than the second sub-sample (Brosius, 2002). Starting ones own business is also illustrated for both samples as a desire to take responsibility. UK students especially agree strongly with this aspect, but again the difference between the groups is only small (confidence interval: UL: -0.314; LL: -0.037).

Table 39: Comparison of fostering factors

German sample			Fostering factors	UK sample		
AM	SD	n		AM	SD	n
4.13	0.923	528	High degree of independence°	4.31	0.790	187
3.95	0.935	531	Taking responsibility°	4.42	0.795	187
3.68	0.995	530	To gain experience	4.04	0.969	188
3.15	1.094	527	Higher prestige – higher status°	3.45	1.060	184
4.24	0.820	531	Realise ideas- pursue own business	4.38	0.792	185
3.81	0.968	528	Opportunity for profit	4.17	0.805	187
2.83	1.175	522	Motivated by acquaintances and/ or family	3.12	1.084	181
3.43	1.065	525	Possibility to put knowledge into practice	4.01	0.782	186
3.08	1.057	516	Good economic climate°	3.46	0.864	186

° Variance similarity according to Levene-test

Similar results can be found regarding the association with the factor "higher prestige – social status". The student group from UK tends to agree slightly while German students perceive this factor as more neutrally. Regarding the factor "Realise ideas – pursue own business" both student groups tend to agree with this factor, while UK students agree to a higher extent. The difference, however, is very small (UL:-0,297; LL:-0,003). In addition, UK students differ from German students, because for them a business start-up portrays a possibility to improve their social status and to achieve prestige. Although, British and German students tend to see a business foundation as a chance to gain experience, this factor is more important for British students. Another difference is illustrated by the factor "Motivated by circle of acquaintances and/or family". Therein, German students tend not to see that this factor illustrates a motive for a business start-up, while British students are more indifferent. However, this difference is again small (UL: -0.478; LL: -0.095). British students agree slightly with the statement that a business foundation is an opportunity to put knowledge into practice. German students have in general a slight tendency to agree with this factor. In contrast with the other findings this difference is more pronounced (UL: -0.724: LL:-0.434). The economic climate plays a minor role for both student groups, however the British students agreed with this factor to a higher extent (UL: -0.534; LL: -0.244).

6.7.1.2 Comparison of Inhibiting Factors

Within the study seven inhibiting factors are perceived significantly differently by students from the UK and Germany (see table 40). Thus, research question 2 is partially confirmed.

German students are more convinced that they have the necessary knowledge to start a business at their disposal. Therefore, they disagree with the hindering factor "lack of business knowledge/know-how" to a higher degree than the British students and the difference is distinctive (UL: -0.908; LL: -0.502). German students also rate the "lack of start-up finance" lower than their counterparts, even if the difference is small (UL: -0.466; LL: -0.127). Thus, they believe that it is easier to get access to start-up finance. Even if both groups rate the "lack of market knowledge" more neutrally, German students see this factor less problematic, however, the difference is very small (UL: -0.411; LL: -0.063). The same picture is portrayed regarding "lack of market transparency". The difference between the two groups is small (UL: -0.489; LL:-0.171), but German students are less concerned. The inhibiting factor "no founding partner" is perceived more negative within the UK student sample than in the German student group.

Table 40: Comparison of inhibiting factors

German sample			Inhibiting factors	UK sample		
AM	SD	n		AM	SD	n
2.89	1.288	519	Lack of business knowledge/ know-how°	3.60	1.180	187
3.80	1.125	523	Lack of start-up finance°	4.10	0.970	187
3.43	1.109	519	Lack of market knowledge°	3.67	0.995	187
3.23	0.948	508	Lack of market transparency	3.56	0.931	181
3.02	1.170	502	No founding partner	3.20	0.999	183
3.04	1.060	516	Insufficient income	3.69	0.967	182
2.36	1.051	512	Lack of social recognition/status	2.64	1.051	182

° Variance similarity according to Levene-test

The difference, however is just small (UL:-0,358; LL:-0,004). UK students also tend to perceive "insufficient income" more negatively than German students. With regards to a "lack of social recognition/status" both groups disagree slightly with the statement. Hence, they share the belief that entrepreneurial activities are in a way recognised and acknowledged. Again German students disagree more strongly with this statement than British students but the differences are small (UL: -0.460; LL: -0.103).

6.7.2 Comparison of Students with Entrepreneurship Education Attendance

6.7.2.1 Fostering Factors

Within the study five fostering factors are perceived significantly differently by students from the UK and Germany, who have attended entrepreneurship lectures/courses (see table 41). As significant differences could be identified research question 3 is, hence, partially confirmed.

In general, it can be stated that UK students tend to perceive the significant fostering factors as more positive than the German students. As regards the factor "higher prestige – social status" both groups would rate this factor as almost neutral in their decision to start a business, but UK students show a tendency to see this factor as a positive effect for business start-up. While German students perceive the possible income as not extraordinarily high or low, UK students are more convinced that they will get a higher income out of business start-up. With regards to the factor "opportunity for profit" both groups show almost an identical opinion to the previous factor, with a higher agreement within the German student sample. British students believe more than German students that a business foundation illustrates a "possibility to put knowledge into practice" and that a "good economic climate" will allow for starting a new business.

Table 41: Comparison fostering factors of German and English students (entrepreneurship)

German sample			Fostering factors	UK sample		
AM	SD	n		AM	SD	n
3.06	1.154	120	Higher prestige – social status°	3.58	1.196	40
3.48	1.012	120	Higher income°	4.10	1.114	41
3.83	0.860	121	Opportunity for profit°	4.29	0.844	41
3.43	1.102	121	Possibility to put knowledge into practice	4.03	0.698	40
2.96	1.064	114	Good economic climate°	3.50	0.874	40

° Variance similarity according to Levene-test

6.7.2.2 Inhibiting Factors

Within the study four inhibiting factors are perceived significantly differently by students from the UK and Germany, who have attended entrepreneurship lectures/courses (see table 42). Thus, research question 4 is partially supported.

Table 42: Comparison inhibiting factors of German and English students (entrepreneurship)

German sample			Inhibiting factors	UK sample		
AM	SD	N		AM	SD	n
2.52	1.193	117	Lack of business knowledge/ know-how°	3.33	1.264	39
3.12	0.979	116	Lack of market transparency	3.51	1.096	37
2.84	0.996	115	Insufficient income°	3.62	1.114	37
2.19	1.067	115	Lack of social recognition/ status°	2.64	1.046	36

° Variance similarity according to Levene-test

In contrast to the comparison group of British students, who have attended entrepreneurship lectures, German students tend to disagree with the statement that "lack of business knowledge/know-how" describes a reason not to start a business. In this factor both groups differ strongly or at least medium (UL:-1.273; UL: -0.351). Hence, German students are more convinced they have the necessary knowledge at their disposal. In addition, German students perceive market transparency less critical as students from UK. With regards to the factor "insufficient income" German students perceive this inhibiting factor as less problematic and tend, therefore, to disagree with this statement. The same attitude can be found toward the factor "lack of social recognition/status". Although, both groups tend to not share the opinion that entrepreneurial activities are acknowledged or recognised, German students disagree more with this.

6.7.3 Comparison of Founding Intention

6.7.3.1 Founding Intention of all Students

The Levene-test for variance similarity was significant on a 5% level. Therefore, a t-test for independent samples with the same variance was conducted. Students from UK and Germany differ significantly from each other. The mean of UK students is 1.01 (SD 1.124) and for German students 1.45 (SD 1.474). Hence, research question 5 can be confirmed.

Both groups are, hence, characterised by a very small tendency to start a business. However, German students show a higher intention to found a business than UK students, even if the difference is more on a marginal scale.

6.7.3.2 Founding Intention of Students with Entrepreneurship Education
     Attendance

The Levene-test for variance similarity was significant on a 5% level. Therefore, a t-test for independent samples with the same variance was conducted. Students from UK and Germany differ significantly from each other. The mean of UK students is 1.17 (SD 1.102) and for German students 1.91 (SD 1.645). Hence, research question 6 can be confirmed.

Within the comparison of students, who have already attended entrepreneurship lectures/courses the result is similar to that stated above. German students possess a higher intention to found than British students.

6.8 Limitations

There are several limitations within the research that it seems appropriate to draw attention in producing this chapter. Firstly, it should be noted that there is a difference in the timescales when data was collected, from the German and UK perspective. The UK data has been collected over the course of one academic year (2006-7), while the German data has been collected over the last three academic years. This means that the UK data will be more subject to the perceptions of the current cohort of students, in terms of the courses attended, the current economic climate and other factors. Further, this has also meant that the German data includes a larger sample size than the UK data.

At the University of Erlangen-Nuremberg and the Metropolitan Leeds Universities two different entrepreneurship education programmes were implemented. The influence of each programme was analysed within this chapter in a way that just the overall effect of these activities on the intention and fundamental determinants was measured. Hence, it is not possible to identify specific parts of the programme (e.g. lectures) that could be mainly responsible for the observable results. Therefore, future research could analyse each component of the programme to find the critical success factors.

The UK sample has deliberately focused solely on students from the Business School in an attempt to compare similar students from both countries. However, it should be noted that the approach to entrepreneurship education in Leeds Metropolitan University is inclusive, and extends to students from across the university. In practice only around 20% of students taking extra-curricular entrepreneurship education are from the Business School, and therefore the impact on such students may well be different to the entrepreneurship education offered to Business Students at Nuremberg where the entrepreneurship education is mainly designed for business administration, economics and social sciences students..

The study did not use any secondary data on numbers of graduate start-ups (foundations) to substantiate the intentions of students, which would of course have their own limitations, for example, graduates may start businesses in different locations and countries and those that can be measured, may not be alumni, or exclusively alumni from the study universities.

As a cross-sectional study and not a longitudinal study has been conducted, no statements and conclusions can be drawn as to whether the differences exists already before the study or whether they were developed during the study. The nature of the cross-sectional study does not allow us to see when changes occur and in which directions changes occur. Future research could analyse with a longitudinal study how the entrepreneurship programme influences the perception of fostering and inhibiting factors as well as the intention of students over time that have attended entrepreneurial classes. Also the entrepreneurial classes could be analysed in detail to identify those components that have a significant impact on the entrepreneurial intention and activity.

Only two universities were included into the survey. The results could therefore be biased due to regional ramifications and future research could include several universities in England and Germany to increase the representativeness of the results.

Finally, within this chapter students from the UK and Germany were compared. However, no gender-specific analysis was conducted. Future studies could examine whether gender-specific differences between the UK and Germany exist.

6.9   Discussion and Conclusion

It is clear from the research that students from each country perceive the world of enterprise and entrepreneurship differently.

Within the study UK students evaluated the nine fostering factors "high degree of independence", "taking responsibility", "opportunity to gain experience", "higher prestige – higher status", "opportunity for profit", "motivated by circle of acquaintances and/or family", "realise ideas- pursue own business", "possibility to put knowledge into practice" as well as "good economic climate" significantly different from the German sample. The factors "higher prestige – higher status", "higher income", "opportunity for profit", "possibility to put knowledge into practice" as well as "good economic climate" were also found significant with the students who had already attended entrepreneurship classes. As fostering factors might encourage, promote and influence or inspire students to want to start a business, it can be concluded that starting a business is perceived more positively by students from the UK and, hence, the possibility to start a business is more attractive for them than for German students.

As with the fostering factors, inhibiting factors might discourage, dissuade or put off people from wanting to start a business. Similarly to the fostering factors UK students tended to evaluate these inhibiting factors more highly. Starting a business for the UK students is therefore perceived as more problematic than for German students. In "lack of business knowledge/know-how", "lack of start-up finance", "lack of market knowledge", "lack of market transparency", "no founding partner", "insufficient income" and "lack of social recognition/status" UK students responded that those factors are most significant in the argument against becoming self-employed. "Lack of business knowledge/ know-how", "insufficient income", "lack of market transparency" and "lack of social recognition/

status" were also found significant within the student sub-sample that had already attended entrepreneurship classes.

The comparison of significant fostering and inhibiting factors shows interesting results. In general it can be stated that entrepreneurial activity is seen as a possibility to achieve a higher social recognition and status. Therefore, the fostering factor "higher status – higher prestige" was agreed with and "lack of social recognition" was not considered as important by the respondents. Furthermore, self-employment is simultaneously perceived by UK students as an "opportunity for profit" and with an "insufficient income". Hence it can be argued, that the potential profit is not a sufficient compensation for the inherent risk of a business start-up. Primarily German students are more convinced to have the necessary knowledge and skills to start their own business, even if the transfer of this knowledge into entrepreneurial activities is seen with scepticism. Additional practical aspects in the entrepreneurship programme or the integration of further entrepreneurs could emphasise the application of knowledge and perhaps reduce this negative effect.

Paradoxically students from UK were simultaneously more encouraged by fostering factors and more discouraged by inhibiting factors to become self-employed, than the German students, independently of whether they had attended entrepreneurship lectures or not. Möller (1998) and Voigt et al. (2006) found that the inhibiting factors in particular influence the intention. This could explain why German students showed a higher intention to start a business than the UK students. This finding therefore offers an important hint as to how to improve entrepreneurship education programmes. That the transfer from entrepreneurial intention to entrepreneurial activity takes place, it is necessary to focus primarily on the inhibiting factors. Thus, the perception of barriers and hurdles will be reduced and the fostering factors become more prominent.

Students can and do wish to engage in enterprise and entrepreneurship education, with the hope of one day starting their own business, in order to be self-employed or to pursue some kind of perceived opportunity. This can be at odds with many of the traditional intentions of university education, which has historically been to produce 'employees' and highly 'employable' ones at that. However, from this research it is apparent that entrepreneurship education provides students with an insight into the world of entrepreneurship which will be useful regardless of immediate career choice, and one which may well come into play at a later stage in life.

The universities that have cooperated in this study evidently approach the delivery of enterprise and entrepreneurship education differently. It has been recognised in the limitations that direct comparison is difficult. However, it is hoped that through collaboration like this and conferences such as ISBE, IntEnt and ICSB the opportunity to experience each others systems for entrepreneurship education are increased, and therefore the quality and effectiveness of such systems are enhanced.

7   Foundation and Development Support for Business Start-ups and Small Enterprises in Germany

7.1   Introduction

The foundation of a business illustrates the first success, as a significant portion of those attempts to start a business fail (Gelderen et al., 2006). Business start-ups and new enterprises are, however, confronted with a multitude of different challenges and problems due to limited resources, insecurities, risks and deficiencies such as missing know-how and experience (Achleitner & Engel, 2001; Dowling & Drumm, 2003). Technology-oriented start-ups in particular have to cope with challenges that result from their innovative character (Nathusius, 2001) and a higher capital demand. To alleviate some of those problems, start-ups and new enterprises can use services and support offered by a variety of organisations and networks. The services and support activities cover variety areas such as education, supply of office space and capital, business plan competitions and co-ordination of networking events and other awards. These types of activities have a positive influence on the foundation, development and sustainment of new enterprises and small businesses that has been confirmed in the relevant literature (e.g. Gottschalk et al., 2007, Voigt et al, 2005). However, the existing studies into this topic are sparse and have generally taken a narrow scope by examining a single type of support organisation, for example Maggi (2001) examined technology and foundation centres in North Rhine-Westphalia. Schulte (2002) compared foundation centres in Germany (Ruhr) and the Netherlands (Utrecht) to analyse whether political expectations could be met. Achleitner and Engel (2003) conducted a survey in 2000 with 65 business incubators (the provision of office or workshop space for start-ups) in Germany.

The aim of this study is to analyse the general environment of the business foundation support in Germany with a focus on an analysis of services offered and the existing network of the organisations.. Hence this paper/chapter aims to identify any shortcomings or problems of the business foundation support offered by organisations in Germany and subsequently suggest proposals for improvements.

7.2   Financial Stages as Theoretical Framework

Greiner (1972) showed that organisations move through development phases in which specific challenges and obstacles have to be overcome. As well as the problems due to development and growth, specific deficiencies characterise the situation for start-ups and new enterprises which can endanger the survival and success of the company. In scientific literature a multitude of different models can be found, that deal with the development of a company (e.g. Adizes, 1999; Hanks et al., 1993; Churchill & Lewis, 1983; Galbraith, 1982; Sabisch, 1999). However, to identify the generic demand for support by business start-ups and new enterprises, it is necessary to examine the early phases of an enterprise in particular, which again have been the object of organisational research. Table 43 illustrates six models of the early phases (see table 43).

Table 43: Models of the early corporate development

Author	Phases of the early corporate development					
Kaiser and Gläser (1999)	Idea phase	Planning phase		Formation phase	Probation phase	
Kulicke (1991)	Prepara-tion	Strategy develop-ment	Concept realisa-tion	Market entry	Market estab-lishment	Consoli-dation
Klandt (1999)	Pre-seed phase		Realisation phase-Planning-Realisation		Early development phase	
Szyperski and Nathu-sius (1999)	Foundation phase: *Target planning → develop-ment of alternatives → feasi-bility study → implementation planning → build up → start-ing business operations*			Early development phase: *Ongoing business operations*		
Zacharis (2001)	Pre-seed phase	Founda-tion phase	Early de-velopment phase	Amortisa-tion phase	Expansion phase	
Kempf and Gulden (2000)	Planning phase	Realisation phase		Build up and start up phase	Development phase	

While these models differ in their structure and labelling, Hering and Vicenti (2005) identified a basic, common understanding of the early phases. They divide the process into five phases: pre-seed, foundation, early development, amortisation and expansion. The early phases are, hence, a basis for identification of deficiencies and problems. To specify these shortcomings specific milestones in the development can be chosen. The financial life-cycle model can be seen as an appropriate framework as specific milestones in the early phases are linked to specific reasons for financing.

Therefore, the financing growth cycle will be used to identify the generic demand for support by allocating the required support to specific phases of the development of a newly founded company. In general, the financing growth cycle can be subdivided into the three main stages: early-stage, expansion-stage and late-stage (Heitzer 2000). The early-stage comprises the seed-phase, the foundation phase and the pre-development phase, while the amortisation and growth form the expansion-stage. The late-stage describes the maturing of an enterprise (Voigt et al., 2006). Figure 24 combines the basic ideas from the life cycle models with the financing growth cycles.

The early-stage portrays the initial phase and can be subdivided into the three sub-phases seed-, start-up and first-stage (Hering & Vicenti, 2005). In the seed-phase, activities before the formal foundation are included, which comprise, for example, the basic evaluation of the business idea as well as the inherent risks and potential rewards. At this time a company in the legal sense does not exist yet (Holt, 1992). The start-up-stage covers the formal act of the business foundation, turning the idea into a legal entity while also establishing the organisational structure including the first links to suppliers and potential customers being forged and the process of product development undertaken (Hering & Vicenti, 2005). The start of production, market entry and first sales are characteristics of the first-stage-phase When the initial revenues are generated (Leitinger et al., 2000).

Figure 26: Life-cycle model and financing growth cycle

Financing phase	Early stage			Expansion Stage		Late stage
	Seed	Start-up	First stage	Second stage	Third stage	
Development phase	Seed phase	Founda-tion phase	Early develop-ment phase	Growth phase		Maturity phase
Profit 0 Loss	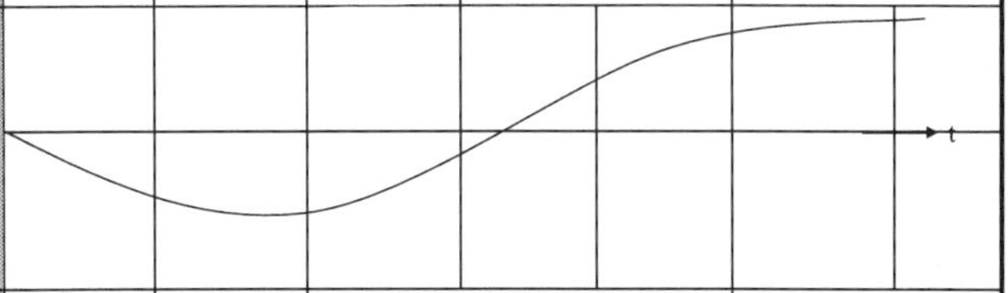					
Financial requirements	Low	Middle		Increasing		Varying
Consulting requirement	High	Very high		Decreasing		Low

Source: following Albert (1994), Heitzer (2000), Unterkofler (1989), Klandt (2005), Achleitner and Engel (2000)

The expansion-stage illustrates the second main phase within the financial growth cycle and can be further subdivided into the second- and third-stage. In the second-stage the enterprise goes through a process that is characterised by an extremely strong growth in order to strengthen the market position and to de-velop the home market further. Therefore, production and distribution capacities have to be expanded and new employees recruited (Nathusius 2001). In addition, the product has to be developed further to stabilise the growth and to respond to possible imitations by competitors and new entrants (Leitinger et al., 2000). Within the third-stage, the company has reached the break-even point (Busse, 2003) and the focus is on the financing of business diversification activities. Therein, new (possibly international) markets are entered and collaborations or mergers may have to be financed (Bandulet, 2005).

The late-stage presents the last phase of the financing phases. The company has achieved the status of an established enterprise and possesses a significant market share with organisation structures having been established and further development potential still exists (Zemke, 1995). However, the company is still likely to be confronted with organisational problems (Greiner 1972).

Within this chapter the focus is centred on the early- and expansion-stage to identify the generic demand for support by business start-ups and new enterprises.

7.3   Shortages, Problems and Challenges of Business Start-ups and New Enterprises in the Financing Phases

7.3.1   Seed Stage

In the early stage business start-ups are often confronted with the lack of sufficient financial resources. Altenburger (2003) argues in this context that the necessary capital supply is not available or cannot be acquired. Huyghebaert and Van de Gucht (2007) give an explanation for the difficulties gaining access to capital due to the lack of prior history, the high risk of failure, a lack of reputation along with a highly concentrated ownership. Hence, crucial research such as market and competition analyses as well as the development of a prototype cannot be conducted. Achleitner and Engel (2001) argue that technology-oriented start-ups in particular have high foundation costs due to their expensive investments in hardware and product development. Lessat et al. (1999) have estimated the financial need for such high tech business foundations in the first four years at approximately Euro 1.5 million.

In this phase inappropriate business knowledge of the entrepreneur can further impede the execution of necessary planning and analysis activities, which can be extremely problematic for the company (Rieg, 2004). Approximately 20 percent of the participating business start-ups indicated in a study conducted by the Centre for European Economic Research (Egeln et al., 2003) that insufficient business know-how was a fundamental hindering factor in the foundation of a business. Larson and Clute (1979) draw attention to the managerial deficiencies regarding marketing aspects as the target market and customer analysis are often not conducted sophisticatedly and found that in 143 out of 359 companies they found a misuse or a non-use of accounting data for this purpose.

In addition to shortages of financial resources and inappropriate business knowledge, another problem for new organisations is a lack of equipment and consumables as well as office space while for business foundations with a scientific background are confronted with the necessity to have access to appropriate laboratories (Achleitner & Engel, 2001). The chosen location for the foundation can also have an impact on the start-up, Achleitner and Engel (2001) indicate that a lack of track record, financial resources and the inability to guarantee a profit from ordinary activities can increase these problems in metropolitan areas.

7.3.2 Start-up Stage

This phase of a new business is characterised by financing and liquidity shortages, as capital is needed to develop the production facilities and to improve the distribution system and as a consequence it may be that the company is not generating sufficient profits and cash-flows yet (Zemke ,1995; Szyperski & Nathusius, 1999). At this stage it becomes vital to attract external investors such as venture capital, business angels or public subsidies (Pinkwart, 2002). In this phase business start-ups can often suffer from deficiencies in respect to the accounting system, a study conducted by Dodge and Robbins (1992) found that 38% of the companies saw the accounting system as a potential problem.

Buhmann et al. (2002) argues that company-specific shortages through can be overcome through cooperation in networks, however, Hering and Vicenti (2005) draw attention to the fact that the company first has to establish relationships to suppliers and customers and that the new enterprise can still be in a weak negotiation position and may miss out on market and industry insights. Achleitner and Engel (2001) emphasise this aspect by stating that the entrepreneurial and business network is in general not sufficiently developed at this stage as financial and time constraints of the entrepreneurial firm can adversely affect the constitution of this network.

7.3.3 Expansion Stage

Due to the enormous growth in second- and third-stage, the entrepreneurial firm is confronted with increasing demands to establish appropriate management and organisational structures (Hunsdiek & May-Strobl, 1986). Hambrick and Crozier (1985) emphasise that high growth leads to a decrease in the quality of daily decision making, "Poor product quality, production logjams, and bad debts are common examples of maladies that occur out of the turmoil induced by rapid growth" (p. 39) Hence, the requirements on managerial skills increase and shortages in managerial skills can hinder the development and growth or worse, lead to substantial risks for the company which Freier (2000) terms "founder's disease".

Typical for this phase are shortages in the financing possibilities of the business growth (Dintner, 2005) and to stabilise and to foster the achieved development and growth, the company has also to invest into marketing activities, the extension of the distribution system and product development. Another problem often encountered at this time is the requirement to begin the repayment of debts (Kaiser & Gläser, 1999). It is for this reason that Kaiser and Gläser (1999) point out that shortages in finance are at their highest in the expansion-stage highest, especially as Nathusius (2001) adds, that if a new enterprise also conducts strategic activities (e.g. acquisition, build up of a joint venture) the financial requirements are rising rather than falling.

7.3.4 Summary

In general, the problems and deficiencies of business start-ups and new enterprises can be summarised in four categories:

The first covers the problems when of access to affordable office space and to laboratory or other equipment (e.g. Voigt et al., 2006; Achleitner & Engel, 2001). Support organisations could offer office space and access to such equipment either at a reduced price or exempt from charge or could request their (existing) network partners to help with this issue. Hence, this chapter will analyse to what extent such services are offered by support organisations

The second category regards the lack of or inappropriate business knowledge (e.g. Bruno et al., 1987; Hambrick & Crozier, 1985; Dodge & Robbins, 1992; Lussier, 1996; Larson & Clute, 1979; Altenburger, 2003; Rieg, 2004; Egeln et al., 2003; Larson & Clute, 1979; Kazanjian, 1988). To reduce this hindering factor training programmes, information material and exchange of experience between the new enterprise and network partners or direct consulting services could be offered as support activities. Hence, it will be examined what is offered by the support organisations to improve the business knowledge and capabilities of entrepreneurs.

The third category is related to financial and liquidity shortages, which are traditionally seen as main deficiency of business foundations and new enterprises (e.g. Beckmann & Pausenberger, 1961; Dintner, 2005 Nathusius, 2001; Kaiser & Gläser, 1999; Zemke, 1995; Kazanjian, 1988; Szyperski & Nathusius, 1999; Dodge & Robbins, 1992; Lussier, 1996; van Praag et al., 2005). Support organisations can help alleviate this difficulty by providing direct financial support or by using network partners, for example venture capitalists or financial institutions. The direct or indirect supply of capital illustrates one of the main tasks of the support organisations. Thus, it will be analysed how support organisations can help overcome financial shortages.

The fourth category comprises a non-existent or less developed network (e.g. Hering & Vicenti, 2005; Buhmann et al., 2002). In this context, support organisations can make their network accessible to business foundations and new companies. Therefore, the network of support organisations will be analysed in this chapter.

7.4   Methodology

The research process consisted of a four-step procedure which is based on the approach suggested by Kinnear and Taylor (1991). Firstly, the identification and concretion of the research objective was considered, then a standardised online-questionnaire was compiled. The questionnaire consisted of mainly closed questions were chosen in accordance with Schnell et al. (1995) and the online questionnaire was designed in a manner to fulfil requirements such as clarity, clearness and simplicity of the questions posed (see Zikmund, 1982; Schnell et al., 1995; Proctor, 2000) with questions based on relevant literature wherever possible. Additional requirements concerning quality factors of online-surveys such as the avoidance of scrolling etc. (Schonlau et al., 2002) were also fulfilled. The structure of the questions was orientated on a procedure suggested by Zikmund (1982) and Proctor (2000) which advocates general questions at the beginning and sensitive or more difficult questions towards the end of the questionnaire. Thereby, the respondent will be eased into the questionnaire so that they can get a general idea of the questionnaire's content (Churchill, 1991) with each topic being treated separately to supports this effect (Proctor, 2000). In order to provide a holistic view of the subject organisations, the questionnaire consists of four main parts: the first part asks for general information regarding the organisation (for example number of employees, year of foundation, legal form etc.)

Next, questions regarding support activities and services were asked while the third part focuses on the network of the subject organisations to obtain information about the contact with existing network partners as well as about the development of the network itself. The fourth part deals with how the organisation is financed.

To identify relevant organisations an internet search was conducted using 11 key research terms that were determined in advance. These terms were "fair", "competition", "business plan award", "award", "initiative", "institute", "network", "finance", "organisation" as well as "centre". All the above terms were used during a second search in combination with the key terms "business foundation", "foundation", "business start-up", "entrepreneurship", "entrepreneur" and "start-up". Form using this approach 615 pieces of contact information were found and subsequently all the organisations identified were contacted via an e-mail which presented the aim and content of the research study and included a web link to the online questionnaire. As a follow up a reminder e-mail was sent every month to those organisations that had not yet participated.

From those 615 organisations contacted 213 had to be deleted from the database during the research process, as some organisations were no longer operational or it had turned out during the research that they did not belong to the relevant research sample (for example private consultancies with the intention of profit-making). Figure 27 illustrates the identified and relevant support organisations in Germany.

Approximately 440 organisations visited the online-platform, however from those 152 data sets could be used for the purpose of this study as during the following analysis a number of organisations were found to not belong to the intended sample (see figure 28).

Figure 27: Business foundation support organisations in Germany (identified)

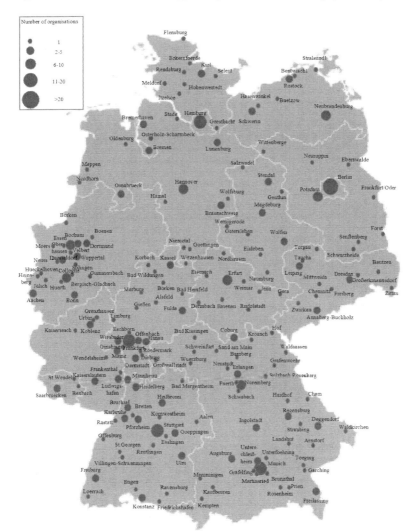

Figure 28: Participating support organisations in Germany

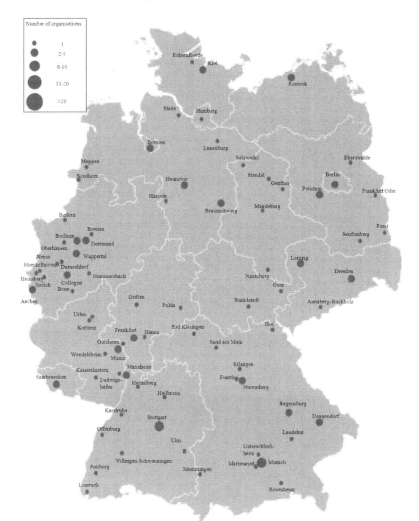

7.5   Empirical Results

7.5.1   General Information

Organisational Characteristics

The participating support organisations have on average five employees and most of them were founded (80%) after 1991. The main financial sources for their activity are public funding (34.4%), revenue from business activities (27.2%), sponsoring (14.4%) and other sources (2.4%). E.V. (registered association) made up 19% of the sample and GmbH (Ltd.) accounted for 21% to illustrate the chosen legal. It was found that 56% of the organisations focused mainly on corporate or technology-oriented business foundations and only few organisations have chosen an industry focus for their activities (see figure 29).

Figure 29: Industry focus of support organisations

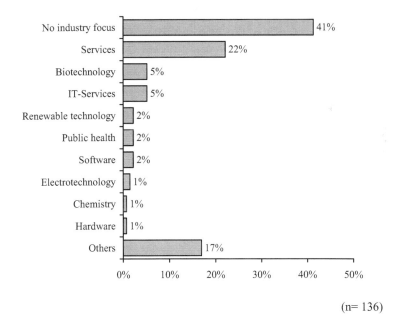

(n= 136)

Regional disparity

The organisations are unequally distributed within Germany with the western and southern federal states (Bavaria, Baden-Wurttemberg, Hesse, North-Rhine-Westphalia) having a higher frequency of support organisations. In the remaining federal states (for example Berlin, Hamburg, the Free State of Thuringia etc.) a concentration of support organisations is exists mainly in the state capitals. In figure 30 the number of foundations, start-ups per 10,000 inhabitants and the number of support organisations are compared. In Hesse, Lower Saxony, Baden-Wurttemberg, Bavaria and North-Rhine Westphalia more support organisations exist related to start-ups per 10,000 inhabitants than in the other federal states although no statistical proof can be given that the occurrence of support organisations leads to a higher number of business foundations, the existence of support organisations and the occurrence of foundation seem to be related..

Figure 30: Start-ups and support organisations per federal state

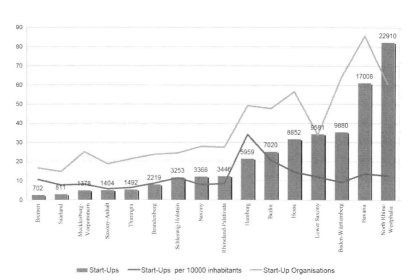

Source: Startuptrend (2008) and empirical results of this survey

Types of Support Organisation

Within this study the organisations were categorised into three different main groups and two sub groups. The main groups comprised start-up network organisations, technology and start-up centres and finally start-up funds. Those categories have in common that they offer a variety of different support activities. Network organisations offer the broadest spectrum of support activities ranging from education and training to the organisation and coordination of networking events and business plan competitions. Technology and start-up centres are mainly characterised by the provision of office space, office services as well as consulting services. Start-up funds concentrate mainly on the provision of finance though public or private capital. Networking events, competitions and awards characterise the sub-groups. Therein, organisations were included that primary and only function it is to organise and coordinate one of these events. The participating organisations per type are shown in figures 31-35. Within the sub-groups organisations were also included with the main groups if it was stated that networking events, competition and awards were organised and coordinated.

7.5.2 Support Activities

Services and support activities have been allocated into five main categories: "facilitation and incubation", "planning tools and consulting", "workshops and seminars", "competition and awards" and "organisation of events.

Facilitation and incubation

Major fields of services and support activities were "facilitation and incubation" as well as "planning tools and consulting" (see table 44). The provision of office space was the most important single support activity with 57 responses, followed by 29 responses for office services and 20 for the provision of capital. 16 organisations offer facilities and machines, IT-hardware and a further 11 licences for software.

Table 44: Fields of operation (multiple answers possible) (n=150)

	Absolute frequency
Workshops and seminars	43
Competition & awards	61
Organisation of fairs	42
Facilitation & incubation	107
Planning tools & consulting	96
Scouting	63

Figure 31: Technology and foundation centers (identified)

(n=166)

Figure 32: Technology and foundation centers (participated)

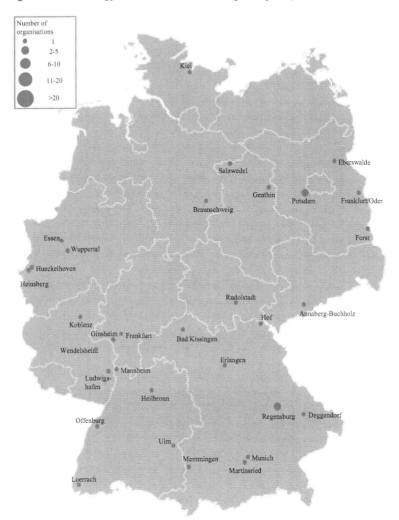

(n=35)

Figure 33: Fairs (identified)

(n=51)

Figure 34: Fairs (participated)

(n=42)

Figure 35: Competition and awards (identified)

(n=126)

Figure 36: Competition and awards (participated)

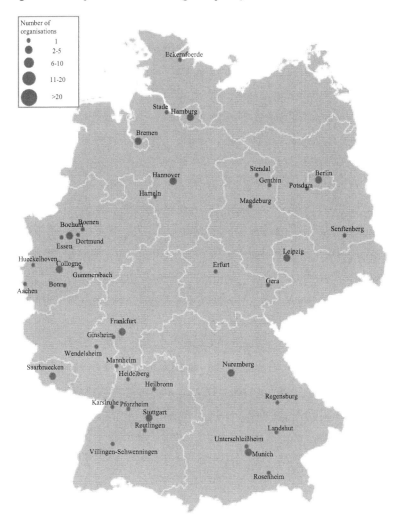

(n=61)

Figure 37: Network organisations (identified)

(n=93)

Figure 38: Network organisations (participated)

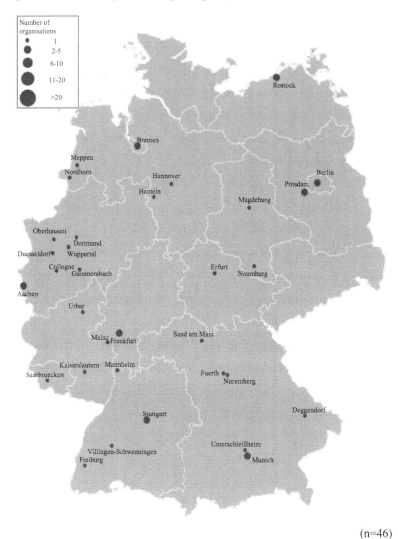

(n=46)

Figure 39: Foundation funds (identified)

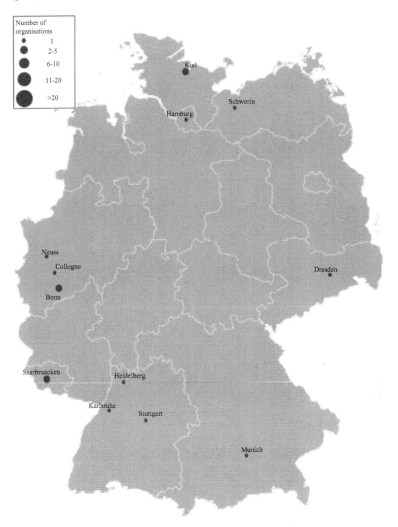

(n=16)

Figure 40: Foundation funds (participated)

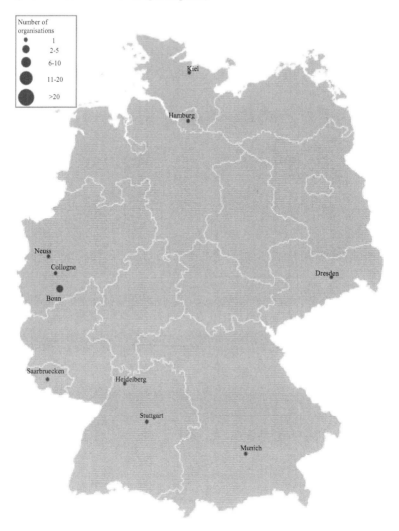

(n=11)

Workshops and seminars

Workshops and seminars tended to focus upon activities such as "business plan creation", "marketing & sales", "accounting & financing" and "market & competition" (see figure 41). However, workshops and seminars were designed to offer topics in all growth phases from creativity techniques to the company's succession. Hence, the surveyed organisations offer support along the financial growth cycle phases with a focus on the seed and start-up and first-stage. We can conclude that, in general, the workshops and seminars were designed to help alienate the problems associated with business knowledge and know-how-related deficiencies.

Figure 41: Covered topics for workshops and seminars (multiple answers possible)

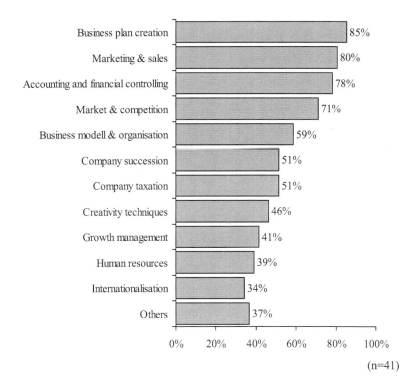

(n=41)

Planning tools and consulting services

Entrepreneurs were also offered support in the seed and start-up phase by making use of business plan handbooks, finance planning tools, templates for business forms, contract templates as well as general terms and conditions. Within the study support organisations often provide a business plan handbook and finance planning software (see figure 42).

Figure 42: Further services by organisations (multiple answers possible)

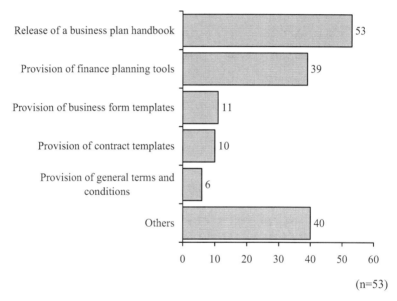

(n=53)

After workshops and seminars 96 organisations stated that they offer business start-ups and new enterprises consulting services. These services range from basic company formation consulting to tax consulting. Company formation and finance consulting were by far the most important consulting activities (see figure 43). ´

Figure 43: Consulting services by organisations (multiple answers possible)

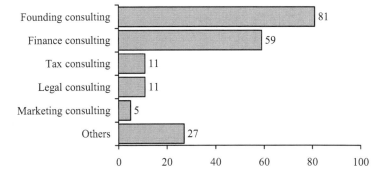

(n=81)

Again the emphasis is on the seed and start-up stage as mainly founding and finance consulting was offered, however, an explanation for the dominance of
these two services could also lay in the legal restrictions in Germany which
strictly control the tax and legal services provided by lawyers and tax counsel-
lors.

Competition and awards

In total 61 organisations responded that they organise a competition (for example
business plan competition or a business idea based competition) or award a prize.
Thierauf and Voigt (2000) suggest that a business plan competition can be a sophisticated and systematic concept to help turn innovative ideas into successful
business start-ups. A business plan competition was run by 31 support organisation, with the competitions being established between 1996 and 2008. More than
half of the business plan participants (51%) were in the pre-seed or seed-phase
and came from academic institutions such as universities, universities for applied
sciences and university research institutions. Start-ups represent the most important single sub-group with a percentage of 22%. The average competition focussed on participants stemming from a supra-regional catchment area, had between
21 and 50 entrants and a steady number of entries each year or cycle the competition was offered (see appendix to chapter six). According to the support organisations approximately 3,500 businesses were founded and more than 14,300 jobs
have been created by participants of the competitions. The prizes were not always awarded against the same criteria, for example 27 organisations awarded a

prize for the entrepreneur, 18 awarded the entrepreneurial concept and 29 awards were given for specific aspects such as development and growth. The spatial catchment area for awards was mainly regional (44%), however 20% of the awards had a federal state and 16% a national German-wide focus. It should be noted that prizes for an entrepreneurial concept or an idea were given mainly on a regional level.

Organisation of fairs

Within the study sample 42 organisations stated that they organise and coordinate fairs. On average a one-day fairs was organised with 52 exhibitors and 800 visitors. The support organisations evaluated the number of visitors over the last few years as "steady" (see appendix to chapter six).

7.5.3 Organisational Network

Often, due to financial and personal limitations, a support organisation is not able to offer the holistic spectrum of support activities and services. Such deficiencies or limitations of the support organisations can be compensated for with a well-developed and sophisticated network of associates and this has therefore also been analysed. Within these networks, the existing contact with companies, investors, economic organisations, politics, the academic area and other groups will be examined in turn.

In the sample, the majority (80%) of support organisations stated they have established companies and economic organisations in their organisational network and more than two thirds of the responding organisations also included contact with the academia and investors. In addition specific relationships with political and governmental agencies were also established by more than half of the organisations (see figure 44).

Figure 44: Network partners of support organisations (multiple answers possible)

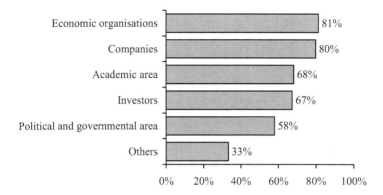

(n=138)

Economic organisations

The category of economic organisations includes the Chamber of Industry and Commerce, employer associations, and employee associations as well as the Chamber of Industry with additional economic organisations subsumed as "others". Within this survey the support organisations had forged a strong contact with the Chamber of Industry and Commerce and the Chamber of Industry, an explanation for which is that workshops and seminars are offered and conducted in close collaboration, and that consulting services are partly configured in a way that business start-ups and new enterprises are transferred from one organisation to another if the necessary know-how or network is not available locally. Contact with employers or employee associations existed even although this was less well developed (see figure 45) perhaps because business support organisations and business start-ups see employee and employer association only a source of information for specific topics.

Figure 45: Network to economic organisations (n=125)

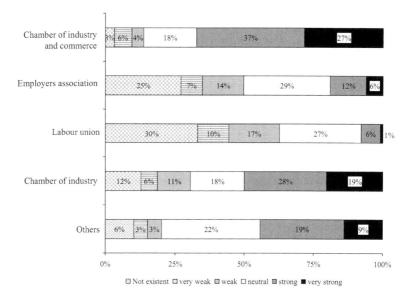

☐ Not existent ☐ very weak ☐ weak ☐ neutral ☐ strong ■ very strong

Companies

Within this study the network relations to established companies and business start-ups are – as perhaps would be expected – quite strong (see figure 46). Established companies can improve start-up support in a large number of areas, for example through involvement in workshops, seminars, experience exchanges or mentor programmes. Network contacts with established and newly founded businesses can also be used to develop cooperation between supported companies and network partners or to help new enterprises forge links to suppliers and potential customers. Deviations from the expected can be explained by the heterogeneity of surveyed organisations.

Figure 46: Network to companies (n=116)

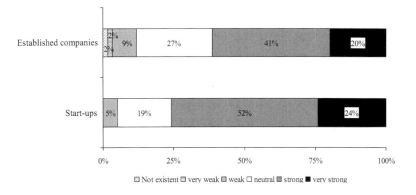

Academia

Support organisations have a well developed network to the university sector (see figure 47) with little difference between the contact with universities (research based institutes) and universities for applied sciences (teaching focused institutes) where more than half of the responding organisations evaluated the network relation as "strong" or better. The explanation for the well developed network can be explained for a number of reasons. For example workshops and seminars can be offered in co-operation and entrepreneurs can use the study programme offered from these institutions. Furthermore, many of the entrepreneurs that make use of the support organisations have an academic background with the majority of participants in business plan competitions coming from the higher education community.

Figure 47: Network to academic area

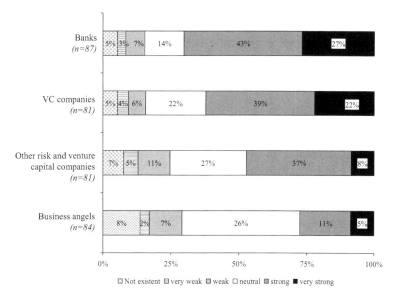

Political and governmental agencies

The organisations in this study evaluated the network relations with political and governmental agencies as "well developed" and "strong" (see figure 48). Interestingly, this is not only limited to the local or regional level where direct contact with politicians and governmental institutions is taken for granted, but also the political network concerning the supra-regional and state level was also assessed by the majority as at least "strong". The exception in this context is at the federal level of politics which was perceived as more neutral. This evaluation can be explained by the fact that many support organisations depend on public money or by the fact that government support represents an important part of their financial basis so it is vital to maintain and cultivate contact. On the other hand it should be note that governmental institutions also seek contact to support organisations in order to foster entrepreneurship and indirectly economic growth through such interventions.

Figure 48: Network to political and governmental area

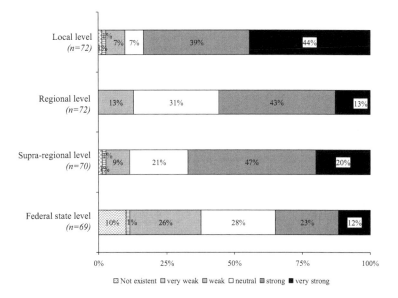

Other network parties

This heterogeneous category comprises groups ranging from tax consultants to the media/press. Within this sample more than half of the organisations evaluated the contact to tax consultants as at least "strong" with a minority of organisations having little or only a weak network relation established (see figure 49).

Figure 49: Network to other network parties

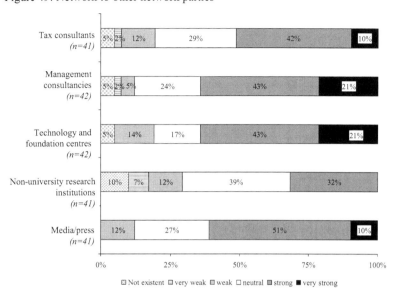

For support organisations that do not restrict their activities to competitions, awards and fairs, tax consultants are an important network partner as tax counselling can only be offered by this group due to legal regulations in Germany. The contact with management consultants is also seen as well developed as alternative or continuing consulting services can be offered by the network partner. The participating support organisations assessed the contact with incubators and technology and foundation centres in general as at least "strong" so that new enterprises can be provided with access to services that are not necessarily offered by the original organisation. The contact with media and press is seen as important in order to generate positive PR for the support organisation itself and its customers – the new business start-ups.

7.6   Limitations

The study presented in this chapter has, however, some limitations. Within this study only support organisations were examined, and not the services that they offer. To analyse the effect of the services future research could consider an evaluation of the services used by supported business start-ups and new enterprises. As a result the importance of single instruments could be compared and fields of development identified. In addition, this study included different types of support organisations which could bias the result. However, support organisations are by nature heterogeneous as no clear differentiation according to their support activities could be made although a single examination approach could compare different types in more detail and thus offer type-specific fields for improvement. Furthermore this study takes only the existence and strength of network relations to different groups into consideration. Further research could analyse the network in more detail to see in which areas support organisations and network partners cooperate to distinguish in which areas improvements could be made.

7.7   Discussion and Conclusion

Within this chapter the foundation and development of support organisations for business start-ups and new enterprises has been analysed. In order to do so primary research was conducted in which 152 support organisations participated. Facilitation, incubators, planning tools and counselling were the main activities provided to support business start-ups and new enterprises. Hence, the direct support of companies in their daily operations is seen as most important.

The provision of office space and rooms was the most frequently offered service by support organisations with only a few organisations able to could offer further business/industrial equipment to supported companies. As resources are mainly limited by financial concerns, it is suggested that support organisations should attempt to intensify their network relationships with institutions such as universities, academic and other research institutions as well as other incubators and foundation.

Within the category of "planning tools & consulting services" the issue and release of a business plan handbook was the most important single instrument for support organisations. Where consulting services were offered to new enterprises, company formation consulting was mentioned as the most frequently provided with just five of organisations offering marketing as part of their consulting activities. Fueglistaller et al. (2004) emphasise that founders with a technical background tend to neglect or underestimate the importance of marketing for the business survival and success so that it is suggested that more support organisations include this aspect into their consulting programme.

Linked to consulting services are workshops and seminars that try to up-skill the entrepreneur. A study of Egeln et al. (2003) showed that approximately 20% of business start-ups indicated insufficient business know-how of the entrepreneur him-/herself as a fundamental hindering factor for the success of a new business.

Hence, the programme of workshops and seminars could be broadened to enable entrepreneurs to deal with business problems more appropriately with to a better knowledge basis. Within our study, workshops and seminars focussing the growth and development of a company were not equal and played only a minor role, therefore, workshops and seminars concerning growth management in general and other specific areas (for example internationalisation) could be fields for further development.

The network relations with the university sector, the political and governmental area, established companies and economic organisations as well as to investors were in general existent and strong. In respect to venture capital companies, this was cited as was strong for a most part of the support organisations, however more than one third had only weak or no relations with this financing group. Due to the importance of venture capital, support organisations could try to intensify the relation to this network group, especially if technology-oriented business foundations are the target group of the organisation.

Regional disparity characterised the existence of support organisations in Germany. While Bavaria and Baden-Wuerttemberg were found to be federal states with a large number of organisations, the federal states in the eastern part of Germany had almost exclusively organisations located only in the specific capitals. Regional disparity is therefore a problem which has to be addressed to enable founders Germany-wide to profit from institutionalised support and thus, to foster entrepreneurial activity and subsequent economic growth.

The existing network of support organisations has some deficiencies that can be overcome. However, in general it can be concluded that Germany possesses a well developed network of support organisations for business start-ups and new enterprises with a wide-ranging spectrum of support activities and services. Within the spectrum appropriate activities and services are mainly offered for the seed-phase when business start-ups are often confronted with the lack of sufficient financial resources."

** Thanks to my student assistants Jörg and Philipp for their support

8   Concluding Remarks

The previous chapters analysed the elements of the social learning theory, organisational socialisation and gender as fundamental determinants of entrepreneurial behaviour. In addition, elements of the attitude toward the behaviour, perceived behavioural control as well as intention were examined.

Matthews and Moser (1996) argued that it is essential for understanding "how interest in small firm ownership unfolds, it would be best to attempt to study it before the decision is made to open a business" (p. 32). Therefore, not entrepreneurs but student samples were chosen for this doctoral dissertation. Woodier (2007) further states that intentions could slowly change over time. Also Matthews and Moser (1996) emphasised that processes related to the business foundation intention are best studied over time. However only few exceptions in the entrepreneurship literature (e.g. Matthews & Moser, 1996; Shaver et al., 1996) can be found which have a longitudinal character. For this reason also longitudinal analyses were included into this dissertation. Indirect and direct effects of entrepreneurship education programmes as form of organiational socialisation on entrepereneurial intention and behaviour have been empirically found by researchers (e.g. Voigt et al., 2006; Peterman & Kennedy, 2003). To analyse these affects within this dissertation samples with a differing entrepreneurship education background were used. In the context of the analysis of entrepreneurship eduacation programmes a need for more international, comparative studies was furthermore identified in scientific literature. Pittaway and Cope (2007) indicated that entrepreneurship education programmes differ in reality within different countries as a result of different higher education systems. To meet this need one paper was based on a survey that was conducted in Germany and England for an international comparison

In conclusion, the collection of study samples wihtin this dissertation paid attention to the factors age, number of semesters, country of study and entrepreneurship education background. In the analysis of the empirical data, attention was given as well to inherent sample characteristics as gender and family background (esp. self-employment of the parents).The focus in chapter two and three was on students who have started their study. The longitudinal results were compared, examined and confirmed with a cross-sectional cohort study. At this point in time the influence of the given entrepreneurship programme at the

Friedrich-Alexander-University of Erlangen-Nuremberg was only indirectly through the established entrepreneurship programme as entrepreneurship lectures are not an element of the study programme. The sample of chapter four concentrates on a later point in time as students chosen in the survey sample were in average in the fifth semester and were subsequently in majority in a graduate equivalent period of study. The influence of the entrepreneurship education programme is thus not limited to an indirect effect, but can unfold its influence via entrepreneurship lectures, seminars and courses that are included into the regular curriculum. Entrepreneurship and business start-up can be even chosen as major field of study. The study approach in this chapter was cross-sectionally. Within the fifth chapter an international comparison with a cross-sectional study between Germany and England was drawn. The theory of planned behaviour argues that the probability for actual behaviour is related to the extent to which an individual intends to perform this behaviour and perceives his/hers behavioural control (Ajzen, 1991). An external factor that can influence the perception of behavioural control and can improve the likelihood of survival and success of a business start up is the existence of a sophisticatedly developed support organisation infrastructure. Therefore, the support organisation infrastructure of Germany were analysed in chapter six. The study sample comprised all support organisations that could be identified via a secondary web-research.

In general it can be stated that the founding intention within the samples was low. Students have mostly thought about becoming self-employment only occasionally. Over time the intention however increased slightly. Especially the intention towards self-employment raised among female students from the first to the third semester. The entrepreneurial intention was, however, in general higher within the male subsample. These results confirm the conventional wisdom that the entrepreneurial intention among students is low and that the intention of males is higher than those of females (e.g. Kourilsky & Walstad, 1998; Wang & Wong, 2004; Scott & Towemy, 1988; Kolvereid, 1996). According to Kourilsky and Walstad (1998), females are significantly less likely than males (62%-72%) interested to start their own business. Also the intention level corresponds to empirical findings. Lüthje and Franke (2003) e.g. report that in their study with a sample of 2.193 engineering students, 44% indicate, that they would quite probably and 11% that they would very probably run their own company after the completion of their studies. The survey of Scott and Twomey (1988) with a focus on university students' career aspiration in three countries (USA, U.K., Ireland) found that the U.S sample aspiring to self-employment was low (25%) in comparison to the U.K. with 41% and Ireland with 34%. Kolvereid (1996) came to similar results in a survey of 372 Norwegian business graduates (conducted 1996). He found that 38% preferred self-employment.

According to the social learning theory the choice to become an entrepreneur is influenced by the observation and evaluation of model's career choice. Especially the family background and the socialisation, which mainly occurs in the family environment, have a major influence and importance on the social learning process. The study results of the conducted studies confirmed this influence. Self-employment of the parents influenced the entrepreneurial intention positively. In addition, results indicated that the influence of the father is higher than the one of the mother. The findings are mainly in concordance with previous empirical results in scientific literature (Scott & Twomey, 1988; Römer-Paakkanen & Rauhala, 2007; Wang & Wong, 2004; Benett & Dann, 2000). Klandt (1984) found in his study that the father's profession has an effect on the occupational decision of the son and the daughter, while the mother's influence is mostly limited to the daughter. Singh and DeNoble (2003) showed that a close self-employed relative has, among other factors, a strong positive impact on the attitude on self-employment. According to DeMartino and Barbato (2003) women are more influenced by the family background to found a business than men. The own empirical results found contrary results as male students were mere effected by an entreperneurial background than female students.

Only a small proportion of students wihtin the different samples had attended entrepreneurship lectures, seminars and courses. The effect of the entrepenruship education programme at the Friedirch-Alexander-University of Erlangen-Nuremberg affected accordingly the development of entrepreneurial intention predominantly indirectly. However, an effect of the established entrepreneurship education programme could be identified in a comparison between German and English students. Paradoxically students from UK were simultaneously more encouraged by fostering factors and more discouraged by inhibiting factors to become self-employed, than the German students, independently of whether they had attended entrepreneurship lectures or not. Möller (1998) and Voigt et al. (2006) found that the inhibiting factors in particular influence the intention. This could explain why German students showed, in addition, a higher intention to start a business than the UK students.

Gender illustrates a fundamental influence on all aspects of entrepreneurship. Gender is a result of biological sex in combination with a different socialisation. The socialisation process starts with the birth and influences an individual from earliest moment of life due to the reaction of the social environment. Hence, its outstanding position is rooted in the fact that it influences all learning experiences (Kolip, 1999) and, subsequently, attitudes and subjective norms. The gender-related socialisation shapes and affects directly the personality. A literature review conducted by Brush in 1992 revealed that male and female entrepreneurs have more similarities than differences in individual characteristics. A similar conclusion can be drawn with respect to the empirical findings of the conducted surveys. The comparison of fostering and inhibiting factors, working-life goals, success evaluation and intentional level between the gender showed only few significant differences. Drawing from data it was found that male and female participants differ in fewer areas than expected. Even more importantly, it was found that both groups showed similar tendencies over time. The findings on potential entrepreneurs are in accordance with literature on existing entrepreneurs that argues that there are more similarities than differences among the two gender (Birley, 1989; Brush, 1992; Green et al., 2003). Identified differences concerned often the evaluation of social aspects especially in the context of working-life goals and the evaluation of entrepreneurial success which were more emphasised by female students. The foundation of a business was perceived by female students more risky than by their male counterparts. In the empirical analysis of chapter four the financial and failure risk was found significant only for women. This is in accordance with the results of recent literature (e.g. Johnson & Storey, 1993; Voigt et al., 2006; Ljunggren & Kolvereid, 1996; Sternberg et al., 2004). Research has also been conducted to examine the effect of gender on the career choice. In the context of entrepreneurship, women have been reported to have less self-efficacy than men (Birley, 1989). Scherer et al. (1990) confirmed this in their empirical study. Barret (1995) added that men were more likely to enter a female-dominated industry than women. Kourilsky and Walstad (1998) used a sample of the Gallup Organization with a sample of approximately 1000 male and female youths. Both males and females showed a low level of entrepreneurship knowledge, but females were more aware of their deficiencies in this context than their male counterparts. Simultaneously, the probability in the female sub sample was lower to start a business. Hence, their self-efficacy or perceived behavioural control could have influenced negatively the intention to start a business. The analysis of the data within this dissertation did not find significant differences in items regarding the perceived behavioural control (e.g. missing business knowledge). An explanation for the discrepancies of empirical findings in scientific literature and own analyses could occur from an inherent sample bias. As students from a business faculty were chosen as study sample the knowledge regarding entrepreneurial activity could be above the average from the general population.

Fostering and inhibiting factors of entrepreneurial intention were analysed within the studies. In scientific literature a multitude of studies can be found that analyses the perception of inhibiting and fostering factors of students (Möller, 1998; Görisch et al., 2002; Voigt et al., 2006; etc.). Möller (1998) found that the important founding reservations were the lack of start-up finance and the high degree of risk. Especially students with a low intention to start an own business saw those reasons as hindering factors. Furthermore, "Too much work and too little spare time" was named as an important hindering factor. Concerning the fostering factors, independence and a better opportunity for self-realisation were named as reasons to start an own business. Within the financial motives, the opportunity for profit was not as important as the financial reward for one's own initiative. Hence, it can be assumed that mainly inhibiting factors influence the founding intention. The results of Voigt et al. (2006) indicated as well that especially inhibiting factors seem to have the main impact on the founding intention. Görisch et al. (2002) analysed only inhibiting factors. The main important inhibiting factor was the lack of start-up finance. Students with an interest in founding a business and those who would prefer an employment status differ in the motive of high personal risk as the latter perceived this factor as the second most problematic while for the former it played a minor role. Similar results were found in the studies of this dissertation as the positive effect of fostering factors as well as the negative effect of hindering factors on the entrepreneurial intention was empirically proved.

Limitations regarding the presented results are predominantly linked to the used samples. The selection of a single country has the obvious limitation that the results can not be generalised across populations and geographical settings. Furthermore, the surveys were – with exception of chapter five – conducted at the University of Erlangen-Nuremberg, which could affect the explanatory content. Another bias could be based on the fact that participants have chosen mainly business administration as their major. Therefore, it would be necessary to include also students from different faculties and universities into the survey sample to exclude study-related and university-related biases. Of course intention can predict activity but it is not activity itself. In a further step a longitudinal study could enable a further look to whether students' intention to become self-employed has become realisation and if not why. If on the other hand intention has become activity it is important to see the quality (in terms of turn over, number of employees, self realisation of the founder, etc.) of the start ups founded by former students. Future surveys could also analyse whether professional working goals change more towards the end of the study programme as the evaluation has a direct impact on the job decision. This approach could help to answer the question when the differences between males and females occur that determine finally the choice for or against entrepreneurial activity. In the conducted studies a rather early point of the life of the respondents was focussed in which only minor differences among the gender could be found. The next step would be a third wave study after graduation and with the start of the working life. It is assumed that the business life reality might act as an influence on the development of different roles in society for males and females.

The results of the studies could have important implications for the practice and the academic research. The result that student's intention to become self-employed is very low should serve as a starting point for academics to rebuild entrepreneurship education. Adjusting the support activities and the lecture contents in a way that awakes the entrepreneurial interest for both male and female students is of great importance. A key role will play the reduction of effects caused by hindering factors on the entrepreneurial intention. Especially within the female sub-sample hindering factors like fear of financial risk, too much work and the fear of failure reduced entrepreneurial intention play a main part in the reduction of entrepreneurial intention. To achieve this goal the entrepreneurship education should become an essential and fundamental part of the curriculum and universities should intensify their efforts in supporting business foundation financially, through counselling services, the provision of office space, (laboratory) equipment and machines or forge links to external support organisations to compensate own shortcomings. The studies have also confirmed that more similarities than differences exist between the gender. However, women tended to emphasise social aspects in working-life goals (e.g. "widen horizon", "work-life-balance", "helping people with work") and in the evaluation of business foundations (e.g. "offered social benefits", "secure jobs", "durability", "work climate"). Jaskolka and Beyer (1985) stated in this context that the evaluation of success has to include to whom and by what criteria a given indicator implies success. Following the measurement of entrepreneurial success could be adapted to the self-perception of success by women. An existing bias in the success measurement of new enterprises could be eliminated by this.

Appendix to Chapter 4

Hindering factors- intention-male sample

Model Summary

Model	R	R^2	Adjusted R^2	Std. Error of the Estimate
1	.230(a)	.053	.036	1.05316

a Predictors: (Constant), social hindrances, lack of pre-start up know-how, lack of interest and ideas, financial and failure risk

ANOVA (b)

Model		Sum of Squares	df	Mean Square	F	Sig.
1	Regression	13.723	4	3.431	3.093	.017(a)
	Residual	246.233	222	1.109		
	Total	259.956	226			

a Predictors: (Constant), social hindrances, lack of pre-start up know-how, lack of interest and ideas, financial and failure risk; b Dependent variable: intention

Coefficients (a)

Model		Unstandardised Coefficients		Standardised Coefficients	T	Sig.
		B	Std. Error	Beta		
1	(Constant)	2.173	.322		6.747	.000
	lack of pre-start up know-how	-.081	.106	-.062	-.759	.448
	financial and failure risk	-.093	.100	-.076	-.926	.356
	lack of interest and ideas	-.168	.080	-.162	-2.099	.037
	social hindrances	.080	.078	.073	1.032	.303

a Dependent variable: intention

Hindering factors- intention- female sample

Model summary

Model	R	R^2	Adjusted R^2	Std. Error of the Estimate
1	.277(a)	.077	.062	.90792

a Predictors: (Constant), social hindrances, lack of pre-start up know-how, lack of interest and ideas, financial and failure risk

ANOVA (b)

Model		Sum of Squares	df	Mean Square	F	Sig.
1	Regression	16.817	4	4.204	5.100	.001(a)
	Residual	202.784	246	.824		
	Total	219.602	250			

a Predictors: (Constant), social hindrances, lack of pre-start up know-how, lack of interest and ideas, financial and failure risk; b Dependent variable: intention

Coefficients (a)

Model		Unstandardised Coefficients		Standardised Coefficients	T	Sig.
		B	Std. Error	Beta		
1	(Constant)	1.886	.261		7.226	.000
	lack of pre-start up know-how	.049	.088	.044	.553	.581
	financial and failure risk	-.226	.079	-.225	-2.853	.005
	lack of interest and ideas	-.102	.065	-.125	-1.569	.118
	social hindrances	.000	.070	.000	-.003	.998

a Dependent variable: intention

Fostering factors- intention- male sample

Model Summary

Model	R	R^2	Adjusted R^2	Std. Error of the Estimate
1	.301(a)	.090	.074	1.02871

a Predictors: (Constant), independence, status, external factors and experience

ANOVA (b)

Model		Sum of Squares	df	Mean Square	F	Sig.
1	Regression	23.640	4	5.910	5.585	.000(a)
	Residual	238.103	225	1.058		
	Total	261.743	229			

a Predictors: (Constant), independence, status, external factors and experience; b Dependent variable: intention

Coefficients (a)

Model		Unstandardised Coefficients		Standardise Coefficients	T	Sig.
		B	Std. Error	Beta		
1	(Constant)	-.419	.387		-1.082	.280
	Independence	.323	.095	.245	3.382	.001
	Status	.032	.079	.028	.399	.690
	External factors	-.006	.078	-.005	-.075	.940
	Experience	.088	.083	.081	1.051	.294

a Dependent variable: intention

Fostering factors- intention- female sample

Model Summary

Model	R	R^2	Adjusted R^2	Std. Error of the Estimate
1	.249(a)	.062	.047	.91136

a Predictors: (Constant), independence, status, external factors and experience

ANOVA (b)

Model		Sum of Squares	df	Mean Square	F	Sig.
1	Regression	13.525	4	3.381	4.071	.003(a)
	Residual	205.154	247	.831		
	Total	218.679	251			

a Predictors: (Constant), independence, status, external factors and experience; b Dependent variable: intention

Coefficients (a)

Model		Unstandardised Coefficients		Standardised Coefficients	T	Sig.
		B	Std. Error	Beta		
1	(Constant)	-.400	.365		-1.096	.274
	Independence	.214	.091	.163	2.341	.020
	Status	-.025	.074	-.024	-.337	.737
	External factors	.040	.066	.044	.611	.542
	Experience	.128	.081	.118	1.568	.118

b Dependent variable: intention

Appendix to Chapter 6

Business Plan Competition Key Dates

Establishment (n=32)	
Year	Frequency
1996	3
1997	2
1998	1
1999	3
2001	3
2003	4
2004	2
2005	5
2006	2
2007	5
Spatial catchment area (n=31)	
Catchment area	Frequency
local	2
regional	10
supra-regional	5
federal-state wide	9
Germany wide	5

| Number of participants in the last competition *(n=31)* ||
Participants	Frequency
0 till 10	4
11 till 20	4
21 till 50	7
51 till 100	4
101 till 150	4
151 till 250	4
251 till 500	3
more than 500	1
Structure of the participants *(n=31)*	
Participants...	Percentage
... came from universities	19.7%
... came from universities for applied sciences	20.5%
... came from university research institution	10.3%
... came from other research institutions	10.3%
... were established Companies	10.3%
... were start-ups	22.2%
Others	8%

Key Facts of Organised Fairs

Organised fairs *(n=30)*	
Number	Frequency
1	21
2	4
3	2
4	1
more than 5	2
Duration *(n=26)*	
Duration	Frequency
1 day	21
2 days	3
3 days	2
Exhibitors last fair *(n=25)*	
Number of exhibitors	Frequency
0 till 25	8
26 till 50	11
51 till 150	3
151 till 250	3

| Visitors last fair *(n=18)* ||
Number of visitors	Frequency
0 till 100	1
101 till 250	1
251 till 500	7
500 till 1000	2
1001 till 2500	5
more than 2500	2

References

Achleitner, A. & Engel, R. (2001): Business Incubation als umfassende Dienst-leistung im Bereich der Seed Finanzierung, EBS-Working Paper, Oestrich-Winkel.

Achleitner, A. & Engel, R (2001): *Markt für Inkubatoren in Deutschland*, Oestrich-Winkel.

Adizes, I. (1999): *Managing Corporate Lifecycles*, Paramus, NJ: Prentice Hall.

Adizes, I. (2005): *The Pursuit of Prime*, Santa Barbara: Adizes Institute.

Ahl, H. (2006): Why Research on Women Entrepreneurs Needs New Directions, in: *Entrepreneurship Theory & Practice*, 30(5), 595-623.

Ajzen, I. & Fishbein, M. (1980): *Understanding Attitudes and Predicting Social Behavior*, Englewood Cliffs, New Jersey: Prentice Hall.

Ajzen, I. (1991): The Theory of Planned Behavior, in: *Organizational Bahvior and Human Decision Process*, 50(2), 179-211.

Alain, F.; Benoit, G. & Narjisse, L.-C. (2006): Effect and Counter-effect of Entrepreneurship Education and Social Context on Student's Intentions, in: *Estudios de Economica Aplicada*, 24(2), 509-523.

Albert, J. (1994): *Unternehmensgründungen. Träger des Strukturwandels in wirtschaftlichen Regionalsystemen?*, Nürnberger Wirtschafts- und Sozialgeo-graphische Arbeiten, 48, Nuremberg.

Aldrich, H. (1989): Networking Among Women Entrepreneurs, in: Hagan, O.; Rivchun, C.; Sexton, D. (Eds): *Women-owned Businesses*, New York: Prae-ger, 103-132.

Alsos, G.A. & Ljunggren, E. (1998): Does the Business Start-up Process Differ by Gender? A Longitudinal Study of Nascent Entrepreneurs, in: Reynolds, P.D.; Bygrave, W.; Manigart, S.; Mason, C.; Meyer, G.; Carter, N. & Shaver, K. (Eds.): *Frontiers of Entrepreneurial Research*, Boston, MA: Babson Col-lege, 137-151.

Altenburger, O.A. (2003): Risikomanagement für Gründer, in: Dowling, M. & Drumm, H. J. (Eds.): *Gründungsmanagement - Vom erfolgreichen Unternehmensstart zu dauerhaftem Wachstum*, Berlin: Springer, 147-162.

Audet, J. (2004): A Longitudinal Study of the Entrepreneurial Intentions of University Students, in: *Academy of Entrepreneurship Journal*, 10(1), 3-15.

Bagozzi, R.; Baumgartner, H. & Yi, Y. (1989): An Investigation into the Role of Intentions as Mediators of the Attitude - Behavior Relationship, in: *Journal of Economic Psychology*, 10, 35-62.

Bandulet, F. (2005): Finanzierung technologieorientierter Unternehmensgründungen: Wirtschaftshistorische und institutionenökonomische Erklärungsansätze von Schumpeter bis Williamson, Wiesbaden: Gabler.

Bandura, A. (1968): A Social Learning Interpretation of Psychological Dysfunctions, in Longon, P; Rosenham, D. (Eds.): *Foundations of Abnormal Psychology*, New York: Holt, Rinehart & Winston, 293-344.

Bandura, A. (1969): *Principles of Behavior Modification*, New York: Holt. Rinehart & Winston.

Bandura, A. (1977): Self-efficacy: Toward a Unifying Theory of Behavioral Change, in: *Psychological Review*, 84(2), 191-215.

Bandura, A. (1977): *Social Learning Theory*, Englewood Cliffs, N.J. Prentice-Hall.

Bandura, A. (1986): *Social Foundations of Thought and Action*, Englewood Cliffs, NJ: Prentice Hall.

Barret, M. (1995): Feminist Perspectives on Learning for Entrepreneurship: The View from Small Business, in: Bygrave, W.; Bird, B.; Birley, S.; Churchill, N.; Hay, M.; Keeley, R. & Wetzel, W. (Eds.): *Frontiers of Entrepreneurial Research*, Boston: Babson College, 323-336.

Baum, J.R. & Locke, E.A. (2004): The Relationship of Entrepreneurial Traits, Skill, and Motivation to Subsequent Venture Growth, in: *Journal of Applied Psychology*, 89(4), 587-598.

Bechard, J. & Toulouse, J. (1998): Validation of Didactic Model for the Analysis of Training Objektives in Entrepreneurship, in: *Journal of Business Venturing*, 13(4), 317-332.

Becker-Blease, J. & Sohl, J. (2007): Do women-owned Businesses have Equal Access to Angel Capital?, in: *Journal of Business Venturing*, 22(4), 503-521.

Becker-Schmidt, R. (1993): Geschlechterdifferenz - Geschlechterverhältnis: soziale Dimensionen des Begriffs "Geschlecht", in: *Zeitschrift für Frauenforschung*, 11(1-2), 37-46.

Beckmann, L. & Pausenberger, E. (1961): *Gründungen, Umwandlungen, Fusionen, Sanierungen,* Wiesbaden: Gabler.

Bennett, R. & Dann, S. (2000): The Changing Experience of Australian Female Entrepreneurs, in: *Gender, Work & Organization*, 7(2), 75-83.

Bird, B. (1988): Implementing Entrepreneurial Ideas: The Case for Intention, in: *Academy of Management Review*, 13(3), 442-453.

Birley, S. (1989): Female entrepreneurs: Are they really any Different?, in: *Journal of Small Business Management*, 27(1), 32-37.

Boden, R. Jr. & Nucci, A. (2000): On the Survival Prospects of Men's and Women's New Business Ventures, in: *Journal of Business Venturing*, 15(4), 347-362.

Bosma, N.; Jones, K.; Autio, E. & Levie, J. (2008): *Global Entrepreneurship Monitor - Executive Report,* Babson/London: Global Entrepreneurship Research Consortium.

Bowen, D. & Hisrich, R. (1986): The Female Entrepreneur: A Career Development Perspective, in: *Academy of Management Review*, 11(2), 393-407.

Boyd, N. & Vozikis, G. (1994): The Influence of Self-efficacy on the Development of Entrepreneurial Intentions and Actions, in: *Entrepreneurship Theory and Practice*, 9(1), 63-77.

Bradley, F. & Boles, K.: (2003): *Female Entrepreneurs from Ethnic Back-grounds: an Exploration of Motivations and Barriers*, Manchester Metropolitan University Business School Working Paper Series, available from: http://www.ribm.mmu.ac.uk/wps/papers/03-09 [Accessed 16.January 2008].

Brawer, F. (1997): *Simulation as Vehicle in Entrepreneurship Education*, ERIC Digest 97-1, ED43346, Kauffman Center for Entrepreneurial Leadership Clearinghouse on Entrepreneurial Education available from: http://eric.ed.gov/ERICDocs/data/ericdocs2sql/content_storage_01/0000019b/80/15/d8/b3.pdf [Accessed 18.08.2008].

Brem, A.; Chlosta, S.; Laspita, S.; Scheiner, C.; Klandt, H. & Voigt, K.-I. (2007): Gender-Related Differences of Founding Intentions due to the Perceptions of Fostering and Inhibiting Factors, in: *European Council for Small Business and Entrepreneurship 52nd World Conference Proceedings: At the Crossroads of East and West: New Opportunities for Entrepreneurship and Small Business*, Turku.

Brinks, M. (2005): *Entrepreneurship Education and Integrative Learning*, Birmingham: NCGE Policy Paper Series.

Brockhaus, R. & Nord, W. (1979): An Exploration of the Factors Affecting the Entrepreneurial Decision: Personal Characteristics vs. Environmental Conditions, in: *Academy of Management Proceedings*, 364-368.

Brockhaus, R. (1982): The Psychology of the Entrepreneur, in: Kent, C.; Sexton, D.; Vesper, K.: *Encyclopedia of Entrepreneurship*, Englewood Cliffs, New Jersey: Prentice Hall.

Brown, C. (2000): *Entrepreneurial Teaching Guide, Kauffmann Center for Entrepreneurial Leadership*, Clearinghouse on Entrepreneurship Education available from: http://eric.ed.gov/ERICDocs/data/ericdocs2sql/content_storage_01/0000019b/80/16/fd/e1.pdf [Accessed 16.08.2008].

Bruno, A.; Leidecker, J. & Harder, J. (1987): Why Firms Fail, in: *Business Horizons*, 30(2), 50-58.

Brush, C.G. (1992): Research on Women Business Owners: Past Trends, a New Perspective and Future Directions, in: *Entrepreneurship Theory & Practice*, 16(4), 5-30.

Buhmann: M.; Koch, A. & Steffensen, B. (2002): Risiken und Strategien zur Risikominderung im Gründungsprozess; Eine empirische Untersuchung neu gegründeter Biotechnologie- und Multimedia-Unternehmen in Baden-Württemberg, in: Schmude, J. & Leiner, R. (Eds.): *Unternehmensgründungen; Interdisziplinäre Beiträge zum Entrepreneurship Research*, Heidelberg: Physika, 137-165.

Busse, F.-J. (2003): Grundlagen der betrieblichen Finanzwirtschaft, München: Oldenbourg.

Buttner, E. (1993): Female Entrepreneurs: How Far Have They Come, in: *Business Horizons*, 36(2), 59-65.

Buttner, E.H. (2001): Examining female Entrepreneurs' Management Style: An Application of a Relational Frame, in: *Journal of Business Ethics*, 29(3), 253-270.

Bygrave, W. (1989): The Entrepreneurship Paradigm (II): Chaos and Catastrophes among Quantum Jumps, in: *Entrepreneurship Theory and Practice*, 14(2), 7-30.

Carland, J.; Hoy, F. Boulton, W. & Carland, J. (1984): Differentiating Entrepreneurs from Small Business Owners: a Conceptualization, in: *Academy of Management Review*, 9(2), 354-359.

Carsrud, A. & Johnson, R. (1990): Entrepreneurship: A Social Psychological Perspective, in: *Entrepreneurship and Regional Development*, 1(1), 21-31.

Carsrud, A.; Ol, K. & Eddy, G. (1985): Entrepreneurship Research in Quest of a Paradigm, in: Sexton, D.; Smilor, W. (Eds.): Cambridge: Ballinger, 367-378.

Carsrud, A.L. & Krueger, N.F. (1995): Entrepreneurship and Social Psychology: Behavioral Technology for the New Venture Initiation Process, in: Katz, J.A. & Brockhaus, R.H. (Eds.): *Advances in Entrepreneurship, Firm Emergence, and Growth*, Greenwich, CT: JAI Press, 73-96.

Carter, N.M.; Williams, M. & Reynolds, P D. (1997): Discontinuance among New Firms in Retail: The Influence of Initial Resources, Strategy, and Gender, in: *Journal of Business Venturing*, 12(2), 125-145.

Carter, S. & Cannon, T. (1988): *Women in Business*, Department of Employment Research Paper 65, London.

Carter, S. & Rosa, P. (1998): The Financing of Male- and Female-owned Businesses, in: *Entrepreneurship and Regional Development*, 10(3), 225-241.

Carter, S.; Anderson, S. & Shaw, E. (2001): *Women's Business Ownership: A Review of the Academic, Popular and Internet Literature*, Report to the Small Business Service, in: www.berr.gov.uk/files/file38362.pdf [assessed 20.08.2008].

Chaganti, R. & Parasuraman, S.A. (1996): Study of Impacts of Gender on Business Performance and Management Patterns in Small Business, in: *Entrepreneurship: Theory and Practice*, 21(2), 73-75.

Chell, E. & Baines, S. (1998): Does Gender Affect Business Performance? A study of Microbusinesses in Business Services in the UK, in: *Entrepreneurship & Regional Development*, 10(2), 117-135.

Chen, C.C.; Greene, P.G. & Crick, A. (1998): Does Entrepreneurial Self-efficacy Distinguish Entrepreneurs from Managers?, in: *Journal of Business Venturing*, 13(4), 295-316.

Chu, P. (2000): The Characteristics pf Chinese Female Entrepreneurs: Motivation and Personality, in: *Journal of Enterprising Culture*, 8(1), 67-84.

Churchill, N. & Lewis, V. (1983): The Five Stages of Small Business Growth, in: *Harvard Business Review*, 61(3), 30-50.

Clark, B.; Davis, C. & Harnish, V. (1984): Do Courses in Entrepreneurship Aid in New Venture Creation?, in: *Journal of Small Business Management*, 22(2), 26-31.

Cliff, J.E. (1998): Does one Size fit all? Exploring the Relationship Between Attitudes towards Growth, Gender, and Business Size, in: *Journal of Business Venturing*, 13(6), 523-542.

Corson, D. (2000): The Eclipse of Liberal Education in the Twenty-first Century?, in: *Educational Review*, 52(2), 111-123.

Covin, J.G. & Slevin, D.P. (1997): High Growth Transitions: Theoretical Perspectives and Suggested directions, in: Sexton, D.L & Smilor, R.W. (Eds.): *Entrepreneurship 2000*, Chicago: Upstart, 99 -126.

Cromie, S. (1987): Motivations of Aspiring Male and Female Entrepreneurs, in: *Journal of Occupational Behaviour*, Vol. 8(3), 251-261.

Curran, J. & Stanworth, J. (1989): Education and Training for Enterprise: Some Problems of Classification, Evaluation, Policy and Research, in: *International Small Business Journal*, 7(2), 11-22.

Davids, L. (1963): *Characteristics of Small Business Founders in Texas and Georgia*, Athens: Bureau of Business Research, University of Georgia.

Davis, T. & Luthans, F. (1979): A Social Learning Approach to Organizational Behavior, in: *Academy of Management Review*, 5(2), 281-290.

Davis, T. & Luthans, F. (1979): Leadership Reexamined: A Behavioral Approach, in: *Academy of Management Review*, 4(2), 237-248.

DeCarlo, J. & Lyons, P. (1979): A Comparison of Selected Personal Characteristics of Minority and Non-minority Female Entrepreneurs, in: *Academy of Management Proceedings*, 369-373.

DeMartino, R. & Barbato, R. (2003): Differences between Women and Men MBA Entrepreneurs: Exploring Family Flexibility and Wealth Creation as Career Motivators, in: *Journal of Business Venturing*, 18(6), 815-833.

DeTienne, D. & Chandler, G. (2007): The Role of Gender in Opportunity Identification, in: *Entrepreneurship Theory and Practice*, 31(3), 364-386.

Dhaliwal, S. (1998): Silent Contributors: Asian Female Entrepreneurs and Women in Business; in: *Women's Studies International Forum*, 21(5), 463-474.

Dintner, R. (2005): Differenziertes Risiko- und Ertragsmanagement im Lebenszyklus von Unternehmen, in: Keuper, F.; Roesing, D. & Schoman, M. (Eds.):

Integriertes Risiko- und Ertragsmanagement; Kunden- und Unternehmens-wert zwischen Risiko und Ertrag, Wiesbaden: Gabler.

Dodge, H.R.; Fullerton, S. & Robbins, J.E. (1994): Stage of the Organizational Life-cycle and Competition as Mediators of Problem Perception for Small Businesses, in: *Strategic Management Journal*, 15(2), 121-135.

Dodge, R. & Robbins, J. (1992): An Empirical Investigation of the Organizational Life-cycle Model for Small Business Development and Survival, in: *Journal of Small Business Management*, 30(1), 27-37.

Dolton, P. & Makepeace, G. (1990): Self Employment among Graduates, in: *Bulletin of Economic Research*, 42(1), 35-52.

Dowling, M. (2003): Grundlagen und Prozess der Gründung, in: Dowling, M. & Drumm, H. (Eds.): *Gründungsmanagement: Vom erfolgreichen Unternehmensstart zu dauerhaftem Wachstum*, Berlin: Springer, 9-16.

Drucker, P. (1985): Entrepreneurship and Innovation - Practice and Principles, London: Heinemann.

Drucker, P. (1985): *Innovation and Entrepreneurship: Practice and Principles*, New York: Harper and Row Publishers.

Drumm, H.-J. & Dowling, M. (2003). Grundprobleme, Ziele und Vorgehensweisen von Gründungsmanagement und Entrepreneurship, in: Dowling, M. & Drumm, H. J. (Eds.): *Gründungsmanagement - Vom erfolgreichen Unternehmensstart zu dauerhaftem Wachstum*, Berlin: Springer, 1-7.

Dunkelberg, W. & Cooper, A. (1982): Entrepreneurial Typologies, in: Vepser, K. (Ed.): *Frontiers of Entrepreneurship Research*, Wellesley: Babson Center for Entrepreneurial Studies, 1-15.

Durand, D. (1975): Effects of Achievement Motivation and Skill training on the Entrepreneurial Behavior of Black Businessmen, in: *Organizational Behavior and Human Performance*, 14(1), 76-90.

Egeln, J.; Gottschalk S.; Rammer, C. & Spielkamp, A. (2003): *Spinoff-Gründungen aus der öffentlichen Forschung in Deutschland*, Baden-Baden: Nomos.

EXIST (2007): EXIST 1998-2006, available from: http://www.exist.de/exist/1998_2006/index.php [Accessed 10.November 2007]

Fallgatter, M: (2002): Theorie des Entrepreneurship - Perspektiven zur Erforschung der Entstehung und Entwicklung junger Unternehmungen, Wiesbaden: Gabler.

Fischer, E.; Reuber, A. & Dyke, L. (1993): A Theoretical Overview and Extension of Research on Sex, Gender, and Entrepreneurship, in: *Journal of Business Venturing*, 8(2), 151-168.

Fishbein, M & Ajzen, I. (1975): Belief, Attitude, Intention and Behavior an Introduction to Theory and Research, Reading: Addison-Wesley.

Freier, P. (2000): Etablierungsmanagement innovativer Unternehmensgründungen - Eine empirische Analyse der Biotechnologie, Wiesbaden: Gabler.

Frese, M. (1998): Erfolgreiche Unternehmensgründer. Psychologische Analysen und praktische Anleitung für Unternehmer in Ost- und Westdeutschland, Göttingen: Verlag für Angewandte Psychologie.

Fueglistaller, U.; Müller, C. & Volery, T. (2004): Entrepreneurship. Modelle - Umsetzung - Perspektiven. Mit Fallbeispielen aus Deutschland, Österreich und der Schweiz, Wiesbaden: Gabler.

Galbraith, J. (1982): The Stages of Growth, in: *Journal of Business Strategy*, 3(4), 70-79.

Garavan, T. & O'Cinneide, B. (1994a): Entrepreneurship Education and Training Programmes: A Review and Evaluation - Part 1, in: *Journal of European Industrial Training*, 18(8), 3-12.

Garavan, T. & O'Cinneide, B. (1994b): Entrepreneurship Education and Training Programmes: A Review and Evaluation - Part 2, in: *Journal of European Industrial Training*, 18(11), 13-21.

Garavan, T.; Costine, P. & Heraty, N. (1995): *Training and Development in Ireland - Context, Policy and Practice*, Dublin: Oak Tree Press.

Gartner, W. & Vesper, K. (1994): Experiments in Entrepreneurship Education: Success and Failures, in *Journal of Business Venturing*, 9(3), 179-187.

Gartner, W. (1988): "Who is an Entrepreneur?" Is the Wrong Question, in: American *Journal of Small Business*, 12(4), 11-32.

Gasse, Y. (1977): Entrepreneurial Characteristics and Practices: A Study of the Dynamics of Small Business Organizations and their Effectiveness in Different Environments, Sherbrooke: Rene Prince.

Gelderen, M.; Thurik, R. & Bosma, N. (2006): Success and Risk Factors in the Pre-start-up Phase, in: *Small Business Economics*, 26(4); 319-335.

Gibb, a. & Ritchie, J. (1982): Understanding the Process of Starting Small Businesses, in: *European Small Business Journal*, 1(1), 26-45.

Gibb, A. (1987): Enterprise Culture - Its Meaning and Implications for Education and Training, in: *Journal of European Industrial Training*, 11(2), 3-38.

Gibb, A. (2006): *Towards the Entrepreneurial University?,* Birmingham: NCGE Working Paper Series.

Ginter, P. & White, D. (1982): A Social Learning Approach to Strategic Management: Toward a Theoretical Foundation, in: *Academy of Management Review*, 7(2), 253-261.

Goffee, R. & Scase, R. (1985): *Women in Charge: The Experiences of Female Entrepreneurs*, London: George Allen and Unwin.

Görisch, J.; Kulicke, M.; Bruns, R. & Stahlecker, T. (2002): Studierende und Selbstständigkeit - Ergebnisse der EXIST-Studierendenbefragung, Bonn: BmBF.

Gottschalk, S.; Egeln, J.; Fyges, H.; Metzger, G. & Rammer, C. (2007): Wirkungen ausgewählter AplusB-Zentren auf die regionale Gründungsdynamik und auf die Performance von ihnen unterstützter Unternehmensgründungen, Mannheim: Center for European Economic Research.

Greene, P.; Hart, M.; Gatewood, E.; Brush, C. & Carter, N. (2003): Women entrepreneurs moving front and center: An overview of research and theory,

available from http://www.usasbe.org/knowledge/whitepapers/
greene2003.pdf [Accessed 11.November 2007].

Greiner, L (1972): Evolution and Revolution as Organisations Grow, in: *Harvard Business Review*, 50(4), 37-46.

Hakim, C. (2000): Research Design. Successful Designs for Social and Economic Research. London: Routledge.

Hambrick, D. & Crozier, L. (1985): Stumblers and Stars in the Management of Rapid Growth, in: *Journal of Business Venturing*, 1(1), 31-45.

Hanks, S.; Watson, C.; Jansen, E. & Chandler, G. (1993): Tightening the Life-cycle Construct: A Taxonomic Study of Growth Stage Configurations in High-technology Organizations, in: *Entrepreneurship Theory and Practice*, 18(2), 5-24.

Harding, R. (2006): *GEM UK 2006*, available from: http://www.gemconsortium.org/down load.asp?fid=579 [Accessed 21.July 2007].

Hartmann, H. (1959): Managers and Entrepreneurs: A Useful Distinction?, in: *Administrative Science Quarterly*, 3(4), 429-451.

Heinemann, D. & Welter, F. (2007): *Gründerstudie 06/07 der Universität Siegen - Auf dem Weg zur Unternehmer-Uni*, Siegen: Universität Siegen.

Heitzer, B. (2000): Finanzierung junger innovativer Unternehmen durch Venture Capital-Gesellschaften, Lohmar: Josef Eul Verlag.

Hering, T. & Vicenti, A. (2005): *Unternehmensgründung*, München: Oldenbourg.

Heslin, P.A. (2005): Conceptualizing and Evaluating Career Success, in: *Journal of Organizational Behavior*, 26(2), 113-136.

Hills, G. (1988): Variations in University Entrepreneurship Education: An Empirical Study of an Evolving Field, in: *Journal of Business Venturing*, 3(2), 109-122.

Hirst, P. (1974): Knowledge and the Curriculum: A Collection of Philosophical Papers, London: Routledge & Kegan Paul.

Hisrich, R. (2006): Entrepreneurship Research and Education in the World: Past, Present and Future, in: Achleitner, A.; Klandt, H.; Koch, L.T. & Voigt, K.-I. (Eds.): *Jahrbuch Entrepreneurship 2005/2006. Gründungsforschung und Gründungsmanagement*, Berlin: Springer, 3-14.

Hisrich, R. & Brush, C. (1984): The Women Entrepreneur: Management Skills and Business Problems, in: *Journal of Small Business Management*, 22(1), 30-37.

Hisrich, R. & O'Brien, M. (1981): The Women Entrepreneur from a Business and Sociological Perspective, in: Vesper, K. (Ed.): *Frontiers of Entrepreneurial Research*, Boston: Babson College, 21-39.

Hisrich, R. & O'Brien, M. (1982): The woman entrepreneur as a reflection of the type of business, in: Vesper, K.H. (Ed.): *Frontiers of Entrepreneurial Research*, Boston, MA: Babson College, 54-67.

Hisrich, R. & Ötzürk, S. (1999): Women Entrepreneurs in a Developing Economy, in: *Journal of Management Development*, 18(2), 114-124.

Hisrich, R. & Peters, M. (1998): *Entrepreneurship*, Boston: Irwin McGraw-Hill

Hofmann, C.; Tilleßen, P. & Zimmermann, V. (2005): *KfW-Gründungsmonitor*, Frankfurt: KfW-Bankengruppe.

Holt, D. (1992): *Entrepreneurship: New Venture Creation*, New Jersey: Prentice Hall.

Hood, J. & Young, J. (1993): Entrepreneurship's Requisite Areas of Development: A Survey of Top Executives in Successful Entrepreneurial Firms, in: *Journal of Business Venturing*, 8(2), 115-35.

Hopkins, T. & Feldman, H. (1989): Changing Entrepreneurship Education: Finding the Right Entrepreneur for the Job, in: *Journal of Organizational Change Management*, 2(3), 28-40.

Horanday, J. & Aboud, J. (1971): Characteristics of Successful Entrepreneurs, in: *Personnel Psychology*, 24(2), 141-153.

Hornaday, J. & Bunker, C. (1970): The nature of the Entrepreneur, in: *Personnel Psychology*, 23(1), 47-54.

Hörning, E. (2000): Biographische Sozialisation - Theoretische und forschungspraktische Verankerung, in: Hörning, E. (Ed.): *Biographische Sozialisation*, Stuttgart: Lucius & Lucius, 1-20.

Hunsdiek, D. & May-Strobl, E. (1986): Entwicklungslinien und Entwicklungsrisiken neugegründeter Unternehmen, Stuttgart: Poeschel.

Huyghebaert, N. & Van de Gucht, L. (2007): The Determinants of Financial Structure: New Insights from Business Start-ups, in: *European Financial Management*, 13(1), 101-133.

Hynes, B. (1996): Entrepreneurship Education and Training - Introducing Entrepreneurship into Non-business Disciplines, in: *Journal of European Industrial Learning*, 20(8), 10-17.

Hytti, U. & O'Gorman, C. (2004): What is 'Enterprise Education'? An Analysis of the Objectives and Methods of Enterprise Education Programmes in Four European Countries, in: *Education + Training*, 46(1), 11-23.

IDW (2008): Informationsdienst des Instituts der deutschen Wirtschaft 34(10), Köln.

Jaskolka, G. & Beyer, J. (1985): Measuring and Predicting Managerial Success, in: *Journal of Vocational Behavior*, 26, 189-205.

Johnson, S. & Storey, D. (1993): Male and Female Entrepreneurs and their Businesses: A Comparative Study, in: Allen, S. & Truman, C. (Eds.): *Women in Business: Perspectives on Women Entrepreneurs*, Routledge: London, 70-85.

Kaiser, L. & Gläser, J. (1999): Entwicklungsphasen neugegründeter Unternehmen, Trier: ProMit.

Kalleberg, A. & Leicht, K. (1991): Gender and Organizational Performance: Determinants of Small Business Survival and Success, in: *Academy of Management Journal*, 34(1), 136-161.

Katz, J. & Gartner, W. (1988): Properties of Emerging Organizations., in: *Academy of Management Review*, 13(3), 429-441.

Katz, J. (1992): A Psychological Cognitive Model of Employment Status Choice, in: *Entrepreneurship Theory and Practice*, 17, 29-36.

Katz, J. (2002): The Chronology and Intellectual Trajectory of American Entrepreneurship Education 1876-1999. in: *Journal of Business Venturing*, 18(2), 283-300.

Kazanjian, R. (1988): Relation of Dominant Problems to Stages of Growth in Technology-based New Ventures, in: *Academy of Management Journal*, 31(2), 257-278.

Kempf, D. & Gulden, H. (2000): Der Weg in die Selbständigkeit - Konkretisierung am Beispiel des Steuerberaters, in: Buttler, G.; Herrmann, H.; Scheffler, W. & Voigt, K.-I. (Eds.): *Existenzgründung; Rahmenbedingungen und Strategien*, Heidelberg; Physika, 51-82.

Kinnear, T. & Taylor, J. (1991): *Marketing Research - An Applied Approach*, New York: McGraw-Hill.

Kirschbaum, G. (1990): Gründungsmotivation, in: Szyperski, N. & Roth, P. (Eds.): *Entrepreneurship - Innovative Unternehmensgründung als Aufgabe*, Stuttgart: Poeschel, 79-87.

Klandt, H. (1984): Aktivität und Erfolg des Unternehmensgründers - Eine empirische Analyse unter Einbeziehung des mikrosozialen Umfeldes, Bergisch-Gladbach: EUL.

Klandt, H. (1999): Gründungsmanagement: Der integrierte Unternehmensplan, München: Oldenbourg.

Klandt, H. (2004): Entrepreneurship Education and Research, German-Speaking Europe, in: *Academy of Management Learning and Education*, 3(3), 293-301.

Klandt, H. (2005): Gründungsmanagement: Der integrierte Unternehmensplan, München: Oldenbourg.

Klandt, H. (2006): Gründungsmanagement: Der Integrierte Unternehmensplan. München: Oldenbourg.

Klatt, L. (1988): A Study of Small Business/Entrepreneurial Education in Colleges and Universities, in: *The Journal of Private Enterprise*, 4 (Fall), 103-108.

Klofsten, M. & Jones-Evanz, D. (2000): Comparing Academic Entrepreneurship in Europe - The Case of Sweden and Ireland, in: *Small Business Economics*, 14(4), 299-308.

Klofsten, M. (2000): Training Entrepreneurship at Universities: a Swedish Case, in: *Journal of European Industrial Training*, 24(6/7), 337-344.

Klofsten, M. (2005): New Venture Ideas: an Analysis of their Origin and Early Development, in: *Technology Analysis & Strategic Management*, 17(1), 105-119.

Kolip, Petra. (1999): Riskierte Körper: Geschlechtsspezifische somatische Kulturen im Jugendalter, in: Dausien, B.; Herrmann, M.; Oechsle, M.; Schmerl, C.; Stein-Hilbers, M. (Eds): *Erkenntnisprojekt Geschlecht*. Opladen: Leske und Budrich.

Kolvereid L. (1996): Organizational Employment versus Self-employment: Reasons for Career Choice Intentions, in: *Entrepreneurship Theory and Practice*, 20(3), 23-31.

Kolvereid, L. (1996): Prediction of Employment Status Choice Intentions, in: *Entrepreneurship: Theory and Practice*, 21(1), 47-58.

Kolvereid, L. & Moen, O. (1997): Entrepreneurship among Business Graduates: Does a Major in Entrepreneurship Make a Difference?, in: *Journal of European Industrial Training*, 21(4), 154-160.

Koper, G. (1993): Women Entrepreneurs and the Granting of Business Credit, in Allen, S & Truman, C. (Eds): *Women in Business: Perspectives on Women Entrepreneurs*, London: Routledge.

Korabik, K. (1999): Sex and Gender in the New Millenium, in: Powell, G. (Ed.), *Handbook of Gender and Work*, Thousand Oaks: Sage Publications, S. 3-16.

Kourilsky, M. & Walstad, W. (1998): Entrepreneurship and Female Youth: Knowledge, Attitudes, Gender Differences, and Educational Practices, in: *Journal of Business Venturing*, 13(1), 77-88.

Kourilsky, M. (1995): *Entrepreneurship Education: Opportunity in Search of Curriculum, Opinion Papers*, Kansas: Center for Entrepreneurship Leadership, Ewing Marion Kauffmann Foundation.

Kourilsky, M. & Walstad, W. (1998): Entrepreneurship and Female Youth: Knowledge, Attitudes, Gender Differences, and Educational Practices - Entrepreneurship for the 21st Century, in: *Journal of Business Venturing*, 13(1), 77-88.

Krueger, N. (1993): The Impact of Prior Entrepreneurial Exposure on Perceptions of New Venture Feasibility and Desirability, in: *Entrepreneurship Theory and Practice*, 18(1), 5-21.

Krueger, N. & Carsrud, A. (1993): Entrepreneurial intentions: Applying the theory of Planned Behaviour, in: *Entrepreneurship & Regional Development*, 5(4), 315-330.

Krueger, J.; Reilly, N. & Michael, D. (2000): Competing Models of Entrepreneurial Intentions, in: *Journal of Business Venturing*, 15(5/6), 411-433.

Krueger, N.; Reilly, M. & Carsrud, A. (2000): Competing Models of Entrepreneurial Intentions, in: *Journal of Business Venturing*, 15(5-6), 411-432.

Kulicke, M. (1991): Ansätze zur Erklärung von Entwicklungsmustern technologieorientierter Unternehmensgründungen, in: *Betriebswirtschaftliche Forschung und Praxis*, 43(4), 349-362.

Kulicke, M. (2006): EXIST– Existenzgründungen aus Hochschulen - Bericht der wissenschaftlichen Begleitung zum Förderzeitraum 1998 bis 2005, Stuttgart: Harzdruckerei.

Kuratko, D. & Hodgetts, R. (1998): *Entrepreneurship a Contemporary Approach*, Fort Worth: Dryden Press.

Kuratko, D. (2006): *Entrepreneurship Education: Emerging Trends and Challenges for the 21st Century*, Coleman Foundation White Paper Series for the Association of Small Business & Entrepreneurship, in: http://labsel.netco.it/Modules/ContentManagment/Uploaded/CMItemAttachments/entrepreneurship%20education%20-%20emerging%20trends.pdf [Accessed 16.august 2008].

Larson, C. & Clute, R. (1979): The Faillure Syndrome, in: *American Journal of Small Business*, 4(2), 35-43.

Laukkanen, M. (2000): Exploring Alternative Approaches in High-level Entrepreneurship Education: Creating Micro-mechanisms for Endogenous Regional Growth, in: *Entrepreneurship and Regional Development*, 12(1), 24-47.

Lazear, E. (2000): *Entrepreneurship.* Working Paper 9109 of the National Bureau of Economic Research, available from: http://www.nber.org/papers/w9109.pdf [Accessed 25.April 2006].

Lee, L. & Wong, P.-K. (2003): Attitude towards entrepreneurship education and new venture creation, in: *Journal of Enterprising Culture*, 11(4), 339-357.

Lee-Gosselin, H. & Grisé, J. (1990): Are Women Owner-managers Challenging our Definitions of Entrepreneurship? An In-depth Survey, in: *Journal of Business Ethics*, 9(4-5), 423-433.

Leitinger, R.; Strohbach, H.; Schöfer, P. & Hummel, M. (2000): Venture Capital und Börsengänge: Von der Produktidee zum internationalen Nischenspezialisten, Wien: Manz Wirtschaft.

Lerner, M.; Brush, C. & Hisrich, R. (1997): Isreali Women Entrepreneurs: An Examination of Factors Affecting Performance, in: *Journal of Business Venturing*, 12(4), 315-339.

Lessat, V.; Hemer, J.; Eckerle, T.H.; Kulicke, M.; Licht, G. & Nerlinger, E. (1999): Beteiligungskapital und technologieorientierte Unternehmensgründungen: Markt - Finanzierung - Rahmenbedingung, Wiesbaden: Gabler.

Lewis, P. (2006): The Quest for Invisibility: Female Entrepreneurs and the Masculine Norm of Entrepreneurship, in: *Gender, Work and Organization*, 13(5), 453-469.

Liles, P. (1975): New Business Ventures and the Entrepreneur, Irwin: Homewood, III.

Ljunggren, E. & Kolvereid, L. (1996): New Business Formation: Does Gender make a Difference?, in: *Women in Management Review*, 11(4), 3-12.

Loscocco, K.; Robinson, J.; Hall, R. & Allen, J. (1991): Gender and Small Business Success: An Inquiry into Women's Relative Disadvantage, in: *Social Forces*, 70(1), 65-85.

Louis, K.; Blumenthal, D.; Gluck, M. & Stoto, M. (1989): Entrepreneurs in Academe: An Exploration of Behaviors among Life Scientists, in: *Administrative Science Quarterly*, 34(1), 110-131.

Low, M. & Abrahamson, E. (1997): Movements, Bandwagons, and Clones: Industry Evolution and the Entrepreneurial Process, in: *Journal of Business Venturing*, 12(6), 435-457.

Lussier, R. (1996): Reasons why Small Businesses Fail: and how to Avoid Failure, in: *The Entrepreneurial Executive*, 1(2), 10-14.

Lussier, R.N. & Pfeifer, S. (2001): A Crossnational Prediction Model for Business Success, in: *Journal of Small Business Management*, 39(3), 228-239.

Lüthje, C. & Franke, N. (2003): The 'Making' of an Entrepreneur: Testing a Model of Entrepreneurial Intent among Engineering Students at MIT, in: *R&D Management*, 33(2), 135-147.

Maggi, C. (2001): *Gründungsförderung und Innovationszentren im nordrhein-westfälischen Strukturwandel*, available from: http://www.meso-nrw.de/TGZ-Maggi.pdf [Accessed 16.May 2008].

Mahoney, M. (1974): *Cognition and Behavior Modification*, Cambridge: Ballinger.

Mahoney, M. (1977): Reflections on the Cognitive-learning Trend in Psychotherapy, in: *American Psychologist*, 32(1), 5-13.

Man, T.; Lau, T. & Snape, E. (2008): Entrepreneurial Competencies and the Performance of Small and Medium Enterprises: An Investigation through a Framework of Competitiveness, in: *Journal of Small Business & Entrepreneurship*, 21(3), 257-276.

Matlay, H. (2006): *Entrepreneurship education in the UK: a Critical Perspective*, Cardiff: Institute for Small Business & Entrepreneurship.

Matthews, C. H. & Moser S. B. (1996): A Longitudinal Investigation of the Impact of Family background and Gender on Interest in Small Firm Ownership, in: *Journal of Small Business and Management*, 34 (2), 29-43.

McClelland, D. (1961): *The Achieving Society*, Princeton: Van Nost.Reinhold.

McClelland, D. (1987): *Human Motivation*, Cambridge: Cambridge University Press.

McMullan, W. & Long, W. (1987): Entrepreneurship Education in the Nineties, in: *Journal of Business Venturing*, 2(3), 261-275.

Mill, J. (1848): Principles of Political Economy with some of their Applications to Social Philosophy, London: John W. Parker.

Minniti, M.; Arenius, P. & Langowitz, N. (2002): *GEM Report on Women and Entrepreneurship*, available from: http://www.gemconsortium.org/category_list.aspx [Accessed 10. April 2006].

Mischel, W. (1973): Toward a Cognitive Social Learning Reconceptualization of Personality, in: *Psychological Review*, 80(4), 252-283.

Möller, I. (1998): Bereitschaft und Motivation der Studierenden der Wirtschafts- und Sozialwissenschaftlichen Fakultät der Universität Erlangen-Nürnberg zur Existenzgründung, Nuremberg.

Moog, P. (2005): Good Practice in der Entrepreneurship-Ausbildung - Versuch eines internationalen Vergleichs, available from: www.fgf-ev.de [Accessed 22.April 2006].

Moult, S. & Anderson, A. (2005): Enterprising Women: Gender and Maturity in New Venture Creation and Development, in: *Journal of Enterprising Culture*, 13(3), 255-271.

Mueller, S. L. (2004): Gender Gaps in Potential for Entrepreneurship across Countries and Cultures, in: *Journal of Developmental Entrepreneurship*, 9(3), 199-220.

Myrah, K. & Currie, R. (2006): Examining Undergraduate Entrepreneurship Education, in *Journal of Small Business and Entrepreneurship*, 19(3), 233-254.

Nathusius, K. (2001): Grundlagen der Gründungsfinanzierung: Instrumente - Prozesse - Beispiele, Wiesbaden: Gabler.

Nathusius, K. (2001): Gründungsfinanzierung: Eigenkapitalfinanzierung durch Venture Capital, in: Koch, L.T. & Zacharis, C. (Eds): *Gründungsmanagement - Aufgaben und Lösungen*, München: Oldenbourg.

Newman, D. (1995): *Sociology, Exploring the Architecture of Everyday Life*, London: Pine Forge Press, Thousand Oaks.

Orhan, M. (2002): Women Business Owners in France: The Issue of Financing Discrimination, in: *Journal of Small Business Management*, 39(1), 95-102.

Palmer, M. (1971): The Application of Psychology Testing to Entrepreneurial Potential, in: *California Management Review*, 13(3), 32-38.

Peterman, N. & Kennedy, J. (2003): Enterprise Education: Influencing Student's Perception of Entrepreneurship, in: *Entrepreneurship Theory and Practice*, 28(2), 129-144.

Petrakis, P. (2005): Risk Perception, Risk Propensity and Entrepreneurial Behaviour: The Greek case, in: *Journal of American Academy of Business*, 7(1), 233-242.

Pinkwart, A. (2002): Die Unternehmensgründung als Problem der Risikogestaltung, in: *Zeitschrift für Betriebswirtschaft (ZfB), Ergänzungsheft* 5, 55-93.

Pittaway, L. & Cope, J. (2007): Entrepreneurship Education: A Systematic Review of Evidence, in: *International Small Business Journal*, 25(5), 479-510.

Pleschka,G. & Welsch, H. (1990): Emerging Structures in Entrepreneurship Education: Curricular Designs and Strategies, in: *Entrepreneurship Theory and Practice*, 14(3), 55-71.

Proctor, T. (2000): *Essentials of Marketing Research*, Essex: Pearson.

Pümpin, C. & Prange, J. (1991): Management der Unternehmensentwicklung: phasengerechte Führung und der Umgang mit Krisen, Frankfurt: Campus.

Rasmussen, E. & Sørheim, R. (2006): Action-based Entrepreneurship Education, in: *Technovation*, 26(2), 185-194.

Reichaudhuri, A. (2005): Issues in Entrepreneurship Education, in *Decision*, 32(2), 73-84.

Renzulli, L.; Aldrich, H. & Moody, J. (2000): Family Matters: Gender, Networks, and Entrepreneurial Outcomes, in: *Social Forces*, 79(2), 523-546.

Reynolds, P. (2007): *Entrepreneurs in the United States*, New York: Springer.

Reynolds, P.; Bygrave, W.; Autio, E.; Cox, L. & Hay, M . (2002): *Global Entrepreneurship Monitor*, available at: www.gemconsortium.org [Accessed 09.April 2006].

Rieg, U. B. (2004): Analyse der Bewertung junger innovativer Unternehmen, Lohmar: Eul.

Robertson, M. (2004-6): *Entrepreneurial Intentions Survey*, Leeds: The Centre for Graduate Entrepreneurship in Yorkshire, Leeds Metropolitan University.

Romano, C. (1994): It Looks like Men are from Mars, Women are from Venus, in: *Management Review*, 83(10), 7.

Römer-Paakkanen, T. & Rauhala, M.. (2007): To Be or not to Be? Children of Business Families Face this Question Many Times Before They Can Make a Decision of Whether to Continue the Family Business Or Not, in: *ECSB 2007 Conference Proceedings*, Turku.

Ronstadt, R. (1987): The Educated Entrepreneurs: A New Era of Entrepreneurial Education is Beginning, in: *American Journal of Small Business*, 11(4), 37-53.

Rosa, P. & Hamilton, D. (1994): Gender and Ownership in UK Small Firms, in: Entrepreneurship: *Theory & Practice*, 18(3), 11-27.

Rosa, P.; Carter, S. & Hamilton, D. (1996): Gender as a Determinant of Small Business Performance: Insights from a British Study, in: *Small Business Economics*, 8(6), 463-478.

Ryan, T. (1970): *Intention Behavior: An Approach to Human Motivation*, New York: The Ronald Press Company.

Sabisch, H. (1999): Unternehmensgründung und Innovation - Gesamtüberblick, Aufgaben, Probleme, in: Sabisch, H. (Ed.): *Management technologieorientierter Unternehmensgründungen*, Stuttgart: Schaeffer-Poeschel.

Sage, G. (1993): Entrepreneurship as an Economic Development Strategy, in: *Economic Development Review*, 11(2), 66-68.

Sandberg, W. (2003): An exploratory study of women in micro enterprises: gender-related differences, in: *Journal of Small Business and Enterprise Development*, 10(4), 408-417.

Scherer, R.; Adams, J.; Wiebe, F. (1989): Developing Entrepreneurial Behaviours: A Social Learning Theory Perspective, in: *Journal of Organizational Change Management*, 2(3), 16-25.

Scherer, R.; Brodzindki, J.; Wiebe, F. (1990): Entrepreneur Career Selection and Gender: A Socialization Approach, in: *Journal of Small Business Management*, 28(2), 37-44.

Schmude, J. & Uebelacker, S. (2001): Vom Studenten zum Unternehmer - Welche Universität bietet die besten Chancen, Frankfurt: F.A.Z. Institut.

Schmude, J. & Uebelacker, S. (2003): Vom Studenten zum Unternehmer - Welche Universität bietet die besten Chancen, Frankfurt: F.A.Z. Institut.

Schmude, J. & Uebelacker, S. (2005): Vom Studenten zum Unternehmer - Welche Universität bietet die besten Chancen, Frankfurt: F.A.Z. Institut.

Schnell, R.; Hill, P. & Esser, E. (1995): *Methoden der empirischen Sozialforschung*, München: Oldenbourg.

Schonlau, M.; Fricker, R.. Jr. & Elliott, M. (2002): *Conducting Research Surveys via E-Mail and the Web*, Santa Monica: Rand.

Schulte, F. (2002): Die Förderung von Unternehmensgründungen in Deutschland und den Niederlanden - Eine vergleichende Analyse mit Fokus auf regionale Gründungsnetzwerke, Bochum: Ruhr-Universität Bochum.

Schumpeter, J. (1934): *The Theory of Economic Development*, Cambridge: Harvard Business Press.

Schwartz, E. (1976): Entrepreneurship: A New Female Frontier, in: *Journal of Contemporary Business*, 5(1), 47-76.

Scott, C. (1986): Why more Women are Becoming Entrepreneurs, in: *Journal of Small Business Management*, 24(4), 37-44.

Scott, M. & Twomey, D. (1988): The Long-term Supply of Entrepreneurs: Student Career Aspirations in Relationship to Entrepreneurship, in: *Journal of Small Business Management*, 26(4), 5-13.

Segal, G., Shoenfeld, J. & Borgia, D. (2007) Which Classroom-related Activities Enhance Students' Entrepreneurial Interests and Goals? A Social Cognitive Career Theory Perspective, in: *Academy of Entrepreneurship Journal*, 13(2), 79-98.

Sexton, D. & Bowman, N. (1983): Determining Entrepreneurial Potential of Students, in: *Academy of Management Proceedings*, 408-412.

Sexton, D. & Smilor, R. (1986): *The Art and Science of Entrepreneurship*, Cambridge: Ballinger

Sexton, D.L. & Bowman-Upton, N. (1990): Female and Male Entrepreneurs: Psychological Characteristics and Their Role in Gender-Related Discrimination, in: *Journal of Business Venturing*, 5(1), 29-36.

Shane, S.; Kolvereid, L. & Westhead, P. (1991): An Exploratory Examination of the Reasons Leading to New Firm Formation across Country and Gender, in: *Journal of Business Venturing*, 6(6), 431-446.

Shaver, K.; Gartner, W.; Gatewood, E. & Vos, L. (1996): Psychological Factors in Success at Getting into Business, in: Reynolds, P.D.; Birley, S.; Butler, J.E.; Bygrave, W.D.; Davidsson, P.; Gartner, W.B. & McDougall P.P. (Eds.): *Frontiers of Entrepreneurship Research*, Boston, MA: Babson College, 77-90.

Shay, J. & Terjesen, S. (2005): Entrepreneurial Aspirations and Intentions of Business Students: A Gendered Perspective, in: *Babson Entrepreneurship Conference*, Boston, MA.

Singh, G. & DeNoble, A. (2003). Views on Self-employment and Personality: An Exploratory Study. *Journal of Developmental Entrepreneurship,* 8(3), 265-281

Solomon, G.; Duffy, S. & Tarabishy, A. (2002): The State of Entrepreneurship Education in the United States: A Nationwide Survey and Analysis, in: *International Journal of Entrepreneurship Education*, 1(1), 65-86.

Solomon, G.; Weaver, K. & Fernald, L. (1994): Pedagogical Methods of Teaching Entrepreneurship: A Historical Perspective, in: *Simulation and Gaming*, 25(3), 338-353.

Souitaris, V.; Zerbinati, S. & Al-Laham, A. (2007): Do Entrepreneurship Programmes Raise Entrepreneurial Intention of Science and Engineering Students? The Effect of Learning, Inspiration and Resources, in: *Journal of Business Venturing*, 22(4), 566-591.

Staats, A. (1968): Learning and Cognition, New York: Holt, Rinehart & Winston.

Stein, K. & Nurul, I. (2004): Entrepreneurial Intention among Indonesian and Norwegian Students, in: *Journal of Enterprising Culture*, 12(1), 55-78.

Sternberg, R.; Bergmann, H. & Lückgen, I. (2004): *Global Entrepreneurship Monitor: Länderbericht Deutschland 2003*, Köln: Universität Köln.

Sternberg, R.; Bergmann, H. & Lückgen, I. (2005): *Global Entrepreneurship Monitor: Länderbericht Deutschland 2004*, Köln: Universität Köln.

Sternberg, R.; Brixy, B. & Hundt, C. (2007): Global Entrepreneurship Monitor -Unternehmensgründungen im weltweiten Vergleich - Länderbericht Deutschland 2006, Hannover: Leibniz Universität.

Stevenson, H. & Jarillo J. (1990): A Paradigm of Entrepreneurship: Entrepreneurial Management, in: *Strategic Management Journal*, 11(4), 17-27.

Stevenson, L. (1986): Against all Odds: The Entrepreneurship of Women, in: *Journal of Small Business Management*, 24(4), 30-36.

Sutton, F. (1954): *Achievement Norms and the Motivation of Entrepreneurs, in Entrepreneurs and Economic Growth.* Cambridge: Social Science Research Council and Harvard University Research Center in Entrepreneurial History.

Szyperski, N. & Nathusius, K. (1999): *Probleme der Unternehmensgründung*, Lohmar: Josef Eul Verlag.

Thierauf, A. & Voigt, K.-I. (2000): Businessplan-Wettbewerbe und ihre Bedeutung für die Unternehmensgründung - Erfahrungen aus dem BPW Nordbayern, in: Buttler, G.; Herrmann, H.; Scheffler, W. & Voigt, K.-I. (Eds.): *Existenzgründung - Rahmenbedingungen und Strategien*, Heidelberg: Physika, 212-223.

Timmons, J. (1978): Characteristics and Role Demands of Entrepreneurship, in: *American Journal of Small Business*, 3(1), 5-17.

Timmons, J. (1994): New Venture Creation - Entrepreneurship for the 21st Century, Boston: Irwin McGraw-Hill.

Timmons, J. (1999): New Venture Creation - Entrepreneurship for the 21st Century, Chicago: Irwin.

Tkachev, A. & Kolvereid, B. (1999): Self-employment Intentions among Russian Students, in: *Entrepreneurial & Regional Development*, 11(3), 269-280.

Ufuk, H. & Özgen, Ö. (2001): The Profile of Women Entrepreneurs: a Sample from Turkey, in: *Journal of Consumer Studies and Home Economics*, 25(4), 299-308.

Unterkofler, G. (1989): Erfolgsfaktoren innovativer Unternehmensgründungen, Frankfurt/M.: Verlag: Peter Lang.

Van Maanen, J. & Schein, E. (1977): *Toward a Theory of Organizational Socialization, Working Papers MIT Sloan,* HD28 .M414 no.960-, 77, in: http://hdl.handle.net/1721.1/1934 [Accessed 15.August 2008].

Van Maanen, J. (1978): People Processing: Strategies of Organizational Socialization, in: *Organizational Dynamics,* 7(1), 18-36.

Van Praag, M.; de Wit, G. & Bosma, N. (2005): Initial Capital Constraints Hinder Entrepreneurial Venture Performance, in: *Journal of Private Equity,* 9(1), 36-44.

Vance, C. (1991): Formalising Storytelling in Organisations: A Key Agenda for the Design of Training, in: *Journal of Organisational Change Management,* 4(3), 52-58.

Verheul, I. & Thurik, R. (2001): Start-Up Capital: 'Does Gender Matter?', in: *Small Business Economics,* 16(4), 329-346.

Verheul, I. (2003): Commitment or control? Human resource management in female- and male-led businesses, available from http://www.spea.indiana.edu/ids/bridge/2003Papers/ZMon_Verheul.pdf [Accessed 09.April 2006]

Verheul, I. (2005): Is there a (Fe)Male Approach? - Understanding Gender Differences in Entrepreneurship, Rotterdam: Erasmus Universiteit Rotterdam.

Verheul, I.; Van Stel, A. & Thurik, R. (2006): Explaining Female and Male Entrepreneurship at the Country Level, in: *Entrepreneurship & Regional Development,* 18(2), 151-183.

Vesper, K. & McMullan, W. (1988): Entrepreneurship: Today Courses Tomorrow Degrees?, in: *Entrepreneurship Theory and Practice,* 13(1), 7-13.

Vesper, K. (1990): *New Venture Strategies,* Englewood Cliffs, New Jersey: Prentice Hall.

Voigt, K.-I. & Brem, A. (2006): Die Person des Gründers als Determinante des Unternehmenserfolgs - Ergebnisse einer qualitativen Metastudie, in: Merz, J. (Ed.): *Fortschritte in der MittelstandsForschung, Münster*: Lit Verlag, 357-374.

Voigt, K.-I.; A. Brem & Blut, I. (2006): *Mezzanine-Finanzierung bei jungen Unternehmen: Arten, Struktur und Entscheidungsfaktoren*, Arbeitspapier Nr. 14, Nuremberg: Lehrstuhl für Industriebetriebslehre.

Voigt, K.-I.; Brem, A. & Scheiner, C. (2006): Entrepreneurship Education and the "Study Cooperation"- Approach - Results from a Quantitative Empirical Analysis, in: *Internationalizing Entrepreneurship Education and Training - Innovative Formats for Entrepreneurship Education Teaching - Proceedings*, Nuremberg.

Voigt, K.-I.; Brem, A.; Scheiner, C. & Schwing, M. (2007): Serial-Entrepreneurs in the Business Foundation Process - Insights from a Case-driven Explorative Study; in: *Strategic Management Society Special Conference 2007, Proceedings*: New Frontiers in Entrepreneurship: Strategy Governance and Evolution, Catania.

Voigt, K.-I.; Mertens, P.; Brem, A. & Scheiner, C. (2005): *Erfolg und Scheitern von Spin-Offs wesentliche Elemente erfolgreicher Gründungen aus dem Universitätsumfeld*, Arbeitspapier Nr. 11, Nuremberg: Lehrstuhl für Industriebetriebslehre.

Voigt, M. (1994): Unternehmerinnen und Unternehmenserfolg - Geschlechtsspezifische Besonderheiten bei Gründung und Führung von Unternehmen, Wiesbaden: Gabler.

Wainer, H. & Robin, L. (1969): Motivation of R&D Entrepreneurs: Determinants of Company Success, in: *Journal of Applied Psychology*, 53 (3), 178-184.

Walker, D. & Joyner, B.E. (1999): Female entrepreneurship and the market process: Gender- based public policy considerations, in: *Journal of Developmental Entrepreneurship,* 4(2), 95-116.

Wang, C.K. & Wong, P. (2004): Entrepreneurial Interest of University Students in Singapore, in: *Technovation*, 24(2), 163-172.

Warwick, D. (1998): Dependent Schooling, in: *People Management*, 4(5), 31.

Watkins, J. & Watkins, D. (1986): The Female Entrepreneur: Her Background and Determinants of Business Chaos - Some British Data, in: Curran, J.; Stanworth, J.; Watkins, D. (Ed.): *The Survival of the Small Firm Volume 1: The Economics of Survival and Entrepreneurship,* Aldershot: Gower Publishing.

Webb, T., Quince, T. & Wathers, D. (1982): *Small Business Research, The Development of Entrepreneurs*, Aldershot: Gower.

Weber, P. & Schaper, M. (2004): Understanding the Grey Entrepreneur, in: *Journal of Enterprising Culture*, 12(2), 147-164.

Welsh, J. & White, J. (1981): Converging on Characteristics of Entrepreneurs, in: Vesper, K. (Ed.): *Frontiers of Entrepreneurship Research*, Wellesley: Babson Center for Entrepreneurship Studies, 504-515.

Wilson, F.; Marlino, D. & Kickul, J. (2004): Our Entrepreneurial Future: Examining the Diverse Attitudes and Motivations of Teens across Gender and Ethnic Identity, in: *Journal of Developmental Entrepreneurship*, 9(3), 177-197.

Winand, U. & Nathusius, K. (1990): Professionalisierungsprogramm für Unternehmensgründer, in: Szyperski, N. & Roth, P. (Hrsg.): *Entrepreneurship - Innovative Unternehmensgründung als Aufgabe*, Stuttgart: Schaeffer-Poeschel, 99-109.

Winter, D. (1973): *The Power Motive*, New York: Free Press.

Wirtschaftwoche (2008): *Unternehmensgründungen in Deutschland*, available from: http://www.startuptrends.de/unternehmensgrundungen-in-deutschland/ [Accessed 14.May.2008].

Woodier, N. (2007): The Impact of an Entrepreneurial Summer School Course on Art Students' Intentions towards Setting Up Their Own Practice, in: *ECSB 2007 Conference Proceedings*, Turku.

Young, J. (1997): Entrepreneurship Education and Learning for University Students and Practicing Entrepreneurs, in: Sexten, D.L. & Smilor, R.W. (Eds.): *Entrepreneurship 2000*, Chicago: Upstart Publishing Company, 215-242.

Zacharis, C. (2001): Gründungsmanagement als komplexe unternehmerische Aufgabe, in: Koch, L.T. & Zacharis, C. (Eds.): *Gründungsmanagement - Aufgaben und Lösungen*, München: Oldenbourg.

Zeithaml, C. & Rice, G. (1987): Entrepreneurship/Small Business Education in American Universities, in: *Journal of Small Business Management*, 25(1), 44-50.

Zemke, I. (1995): Die Unternehmensverfassung von Beteiligungskapitalgesellschaften: Analyse des institutionellen Designs deutscher Venture Capital-Gesellschaften, Wiesbaden: Dt. Universitätsverlag.

Ziegerer, M. (1993): Firmengründungen durch Frauen und Männer im Zeitablauf; Unterschiede – Gleichheiten – Konsequenzen, Disseration, St. Gallen.

Zikmund, W. (1982): *Exploring Marketing Research*, Chicago: Dryden.